PREFACE BY JOHN
Chief Executive of Water

From its construction in the mid 18th century, the Grand Canal of Ireland served as a vital arterial route for passengers and commodities for almost 200 years. Today it is transformed into a vibrant recreational resource for its 21st century users and is an invaluable industrial, archaeological and environmental legacy.

Waterways Ireland has been responsible for the management, maintenance, development and restoration of seven of Ireland's inland navigable waterways, including the Grand Canal since 1999. Over that time, it has developed facilities and carried out maintenance along the canal, with the aim of maximising its potential as a high quality recreational asset, for a diverse range of users and leisure activities; activities that generate significant economic, health and social benefit along the canal corridor.

The Dublin terminus of the Grand Canal is Ringsend Basin where it meets the River Liffey. The canal passes westwards along the Circular Line through the city, before following the Main Line for 125km through Ireland's rural heartland, to join with the River Shannon. It meets too with the picturesque River Barrow, via the 45km stretch of the Barrow Line, as it journeys south from Lowtown to Athy. These linkages enhance the scope and variety for canal users in their water-based journeys.

This new edition of the guide is based on the 1999 edition of the Guide to the Grand Canal of Ireland, which was produced by the Department of Arts, Heritage, Gaeltacht and the Islands. It is intended not only to provide information of use to the boater but also to a wider range of other users of the waterways, including walkers, anglers, cyclists and canoeists. The guide has been updated in conjunction with the Inland Waterways Association of Ireland, with gratefully received assistance from many other sources.

So however you choose to enjoy the wonderful Grand Canal, this guide will inform and advise you on your visit to this most interesting waterway.

PREFACE BY GREGORY WHELAN

President of the Inland Waterways Association of Ireland

The first trade boat passed through the Grand Canal from the River Shannon in 1804, the year after the canal to the Shannon was completed. Since then many boats have journeyed along the Grand Canal for both trade and pleasure.

The first edition of the Guide to the Grand Canal was published by the Inland Waterways Association of Ireland (IWAI) under the editorship of Ruth Delany and Jeremy Addis in 1975.

This edition of Guide to the Grand Canal of Ireland includes significant changes, the text and maps have been fully updated and the guide also takes into account updated facilities adjacent to the canal, developments along the canal and new and upgraded canal infrastructure along with navigation advice and lock keeper contacts etc.

In reviewing this edition, I cannot but reflect on how many of the changes in the guide provide a snap shot of general society changes over the past three decades with new infrastructure combined with changing industrial heritage, commercial and social entities. Indeed the point at where the canal emerges into a country setting is getting further and further away from Ringsend with each edition of the guide. Over 200 years in existence the Grand Canal continues to provide an economic function as it moves to its new commerce of tourism, a joy for new users both afloat and ashore.

The Association is grateful to the generous work of IWAI members John Dolan, Mick Farrell, Gerry Burke, the four IWAI Grand Canal branches and their families and boating friends, in preparing this edition, Waterways Ireland our fellow publisher on the guide and the other agencies involved in preparing this edition.

CONTENTS

PUBLISHED BY WATERWAYS IRELAND IN ASSOCIATION WITH
THE INLAND WATERWAYS ASSOCIATION OF IRELAND (IWAI)

© Copyright of Maps and Content: Waterways Ireland and Inland Waterways Association of
Ireland

ISBN: 978-0-9564994-4-8

Disclaimer: While every effort has been made to ensure accuracy in the information supplied,
no responsibility can be accepted for any damage or loss suffered as a result of error, omission
or misinterpretation of this information.

NAVIGATING THE GRAND CANAL

Built amid the 19th Century canal fever that swept across Ireland, the Grand Canal stretches across the country, from Dublin to the Shannon. From its historic origins, when horse-drawn barges originally travelled this water route, the canal today has emerged as a relaxing haven for anyone seeking a leisurely pace and the secluded spots along its banks. From its terminus at Ringsend Basin, the canal follows the Circular Line and enters the heart of Dublin through Inchicore. The city canal stretches offer close access to the museums and galleries, theatres, shopping and nightlife. Travelling by boat outside Dublin offers you the option to change your scenery, as the canal passes through more rural countryside, with the small towns and villages that line the canal providing a different type of entertainment. This guide will provide you with the information you need for navigating the Grand Canal.

Navigation Authority

The Grand Canal and the Barrow Line of the Grand Canal are managed by Waterways Ireland Eastern Regional Office which is located at:

Floor 2 Block C, Ashtowngate, Navan Road, Dublin 15
Tel: +353 (0)1 868 0148   **Fax:** +353 (0)1 838 3647

Full information regarding Waterways Ireland's role and responsibilities as the navigation authority for the inland waterways can be found by accessing the website at www.waterwaysireland.org
Queries can be directed by email to info@waterwaysireland.org

The Grand Canal and Barrow Line of the Grand Canal

The Main Line of the Grand Canal crosses Leinster from Ringsend in Dublin City to the River Shannon at Shannon Harbour in County Offaly. It is 131km long with 43 locks, five of which are doubles. There are in addition three sea-locks linking the Grand Canal Basin in Ringsend with the tidal River Liffey. The Barrow Line (45km and nine locks, including two doubles) runs south from the summit level at Lowtown in Co Kildare to join the River Barrow in Athy. The Naas Branch is navigable to Naas Harbour (4km with 5 single locks) but a low bridge blocks the navigation from there to the old harbour at Corbally, 8km away. The Kilbeggan Branch was closed to navigation in 1961, although there is a walking path along it. The Kilbeggan Harbour Amenity Group and Ballycommon Canal Renewal Group are working to have this branch restored.

Navigation Criteria

Navigation is not allowed between the hours of sunset and sunrise. Maximum dimensions of craft permitted to use the Grand Canal are as below. These are given as a guide only and cannot be guaranteed, particularly during periods when water levels are low. Lowest bridge on the Grand Canal is the Ringsend Railway Bridge.

- Length   18.50m
- Beam   3.90m
- Draft   1.20m
- Height over water (airdraft) 2.45m over a width of 3.00m

Permits

On the Grand Canal, including the Barrow Line, all boats must show a valid permit. A Combined Mooring and Passage Permit (CMP), which allows for

mooring within the five-day rule and unlimited lock passage for twelve months, currently costs €126. An Extended Mooring Permit (EMP) is also needed for any boat owner wishing to moor their boat for longer than five days in one location. These moorings are at certain designated locations on the canal and this Extended Mooring Permit currently costs €152 per year. The Extended Mooring Permit is only available if a Combined Mooring and Passage Permit is also held.

Applications for permits should be made to Waterways Ireland Inspectorate at Harbour Street, Tullamore, Co Offaly **Tel:** +353 (0)57 935 2300. Permit Application Forms may also be downloaded from www.waterwaysireland.org or obtained from Waterways Ireland Eastern Regional Office, Dublin **Tel:** +353 (0)1 868 0148 or from any of the Lockkeepers located on the Grand Canal and Barrow Line (contact telephone numbers for all Lockkeepers are provided in the next section, *Operating Locks*).

Traffic

The general rule is that traffic should keep to the right, but when navigation is clear ahead, travel towards the centre of the canal. Take extreme care and reduce speed appropriately when approaching bends and bridges etc. If the view of the navigation ahead is blocked, keep to the right taking due recognition of the depths available. Some locations are narrow and should be navigated with care, particularly when passing or overtaking other boats.

The maximum speed on the canal is 6km/h and damage to the banks results from speeds in excess of this.

Watch your Wash - engine propelled crafts all create a wake behind them. A fast flow of water from the stern of the craft can cause excessive wash which has the potential to cause significant disturbance to other canal users and the destruction of birds' nests in the reeds, the bank habitat and also bank erosion. Where safe, users should reduce speed to prevent the above and slow down where boats are moored, or when approaching locks, jetties, fishermen, other waterways users and where water activities are underway.

Opening Hours of Locks

Daylight Hours, however Lockkeeper attendance not available during all of these hours so it is advisable to contact Lockkeepers in advance to confirm availability. The sea-lock requires attendance by the Dock Superintendent to make passage **Tel:** +353 (0)87 258 4713 and Locks 1-12 Main Line require prior notice to the Eastern Regional Office **Tel:** +353 (0)1 868 0148. Occasionally locks and/or stretches of the canal will be closed or navigation restricted and these will be notified by Marine Notice, visit **www.waterwaysireland.org**

Moorings

Under the Canals Act (1986) Bye-laws (1988), a boat can moor at the same public mooring or within 500m of the same place for a maximum of 5 days, or longer if a valid EMP is held (see Permits section). Care should be taken when mooring, vessels should not be tied up at locks, pump-out stations or so that they obstruct navigation or safe use of facilities.

Waiting Jetties

Waiting Jetties are provided at locks or bridges to facilitate navigation through the area and are not for longer term mooring.

Services

Service blocks with showers and toilets are located at Lowtown and at Shannon Harbour. The service block at Shannon Harbour also has a laundry facility. Pump-outs are available adjacent to both of these service blocks and also at Tullamore, Edenderry and Athy. Smart Cards are used to operate the service blocks or pump-outs and can be purchased from Waterways Ireland Offices, local outlets, or the Lockkeepers at Lowtown, Shannon Harbour and Monasterevin (Barrow Line). A full listing of stockists is available on the website **www.waterwaysireland.org**

Slipways

There are slipways at:-

- Grand Canal Dock/Ringsend Basin (contact Dock Superintendent in advance)
- 9th Lock, Clondalkin (contact Lockkeeper in advance)
- Robertstown
- George's Bridge (Edenderry)
- Waterways Ireland Depot, Tullamore Harbour (office hours only)
- Rathangan Bridge
- Monasterevin (Moore's Bridge)

Dry Docks

Dry docks are available at Shannon Harbour and at the Waterways Ireland depot in Tullamore. Contact the Tullamore office to reserve these facilities **Tel:** +353 (0)57 935 2300.

Fuel

Fuel is available from garages adjacent to the canal. Bring your own containers and ensure no spillage.

Safety

Ensure that boats have sufficient crew to handle them effectively. In line with legislative requirements under Statutory Instrument (S.I.) number 259/2004, Waterways Ireland advises all users of the navigation to wear a lifejacket at all times while on board. It is the law that all children under the age of 16 must wear a suitable life jacket and that all vessels should have sufficient, suitable lifejackets on board for all crew and boat passengers

Lock chambers are not equipped with ladders or lifebuoys. Swimming is not allowed in any lock, harbour or dock.

Health

The quality of water in the canal is generally good but, unlike tap water, it is untreated and micro-organisms are naturally present. The risk of contracting illness (including Weil's Disease) is small but you should take sensible precautions:-

* cover any cuts with a waterproof dressing
* wash with clean water after canal activities
* if you become ill within two weeks, let your doctor know that you have been in contact with untreated water

Entrance to the Grand Canal from the Sea

Entrance to the Grand Canal from the Irish Sea is via the River Liffey and the Buckingham Sea-Lock at Ringsend. Currently Grand Canal Basin is only open to craft intending to travel the Grand Canal (see the navigation dimensions for the canal). To reserve a passage through the sea-lock and for further information contact the Dock Superintendent **Tel:** +353 (0)87 258 4713.

Information and guidance on entering Dublin Port is available from Dublin Port.

Dublin Port Company, Port Centre, Alexandra Road, Dublin 1

Tel: +353 (0)1 887 6000
Email: info@dublinport.ie
Web: www.dublinport.ie

Locks 1 to 12

Locks 1 to 12 on the Grand Canal connect the Circular Line at Inchicore to the edge of the city near Lucan, a distance of 10km and a rise of 45m through nine single locks and three double locks. Navigation on this Dublin stretch of the canal is subject to special conditions and is only permissible by prior arrangement. Passage is organised directly through the Eastern Regional Office, generally to be undertaken over the course of a morning. Contact the office **Tel:** +353 (0)1 868 0148 with a minimum of two days notice to arrange passage in or out of Dublin through these locks.

For further information on navigating and boat queries contact the Waterways Ireland Inspectorate:

Inspector of Navigation
Waterways Ireland, The Docks, Athlone, Co Westmeath
Tel: +353 (0)90 649 4232

Assistant Inspector of Navigation
Waterways Ireland, Harbour Street, Tullamore, Co Offaly
Tel: +353 (0)57 935 2300

Maintenance Works

Any scheduled maintenance works are generally carried out by Waterways Ireland between 1st November and 17th March. If making a journey during this time, contact Waterways Ireland Operations at Eastern Regional Office **Tel:** +353 (0)1 868 0148.

Alternatively visit **www.waterwaysireland.org** or **www.iwai.ie** for Marine Notices.

Navigation Legislation

The following navigation legislation applies to the Grand Canal at the time of publishing:-

* Canals Act 1986, Canals Act 1986 (Bye-Laws 1988)
* Merchant Shipping (Mechanically Propelled Pleasure Craft) (Safety) Regulations 2001
* Merchant Shipping (Pleasure Craft) (Lifejackets and Operation) (Safety) Regulations 2004
* International Regulations for Preventing Collisions at Sea 1972 (COLREGS).
* Martime Safety Act 2005

Legislation is available online at **www.irishstatutebook.ie**

Maps

Ordnance Survey (Discovery Series) 1:50,000 sheets numbers 47, 48, 49, 50 & 55.

Public Transport

It should be noted that in more remote areas the services tend to be very infrequent, no more than one or two buses per day in each direction. Reference should be made to the Dublin Bus **www.dublinbus.ie** or Bus Éireann Expressway & Local Bus Timetables **www.buseireann.ie** for full information. There are also train services from major towns **www.irishrail.ie**

Further Reading

Ireland's Inland Waterways (Revised ed.) by Ruth Delany, published in 1993. Covers the history of all of Ireland's canals and river navigations.

The Grand Canal of Ireland (2nd ed.) by Ruth Delany, published by the Office of Public Works and Lilliput Press, 1995. (1st ed. published by David & Charles, 1973).

In the Wake of Giants, Journeys on the Barrow and the Grand Canal by Gerald Potterton, published by Cottage Publications, 2008.

Green and Silver, (3rd ed.) by L.T.C. Rolt, published in 1993 by Athlone Branch IWAI.

The Grand Canal in Inchicore and Kilmainham, complied by the Inchicore and Kilmainham Development Project, (2nd ed.) Sponsored by the Office of Public Works, published in 1994.

OPERATING LOCKS

Introduction

The locks on the Grand Canal, with the exception of the sea-lock from the Liffey, are operated manually and require a lock-key. The assistance of a Lockkeeper can be requested by direct phone contact with the individual Lockkeeper. The process is outlined on the following pages but operating locks requires some guidance initially. Boat owners interested in putting a boat on the canal should contact Waterways Ireland Eastern Regional Office to make the necessary arrangements.

Eastern Regional Office **Tel:** +353 (0)1 868 0148

When assistance with boat movement is required thereafter, you should contact the appropriate Lockkeeper as per the contacts on the following pages. Observe the correct procedure when passing your boat through the lock. The inexperienced should use lock gear extremely cautiously; nothing should be done unless you understand the consequences. In good order, lock racks and gates do not need much force to operate.

For boats intending to travel through Main Line Locks 1 - 12, two days prior notice must be given to the Eastern Regional Office who will then arrange passage and inform the relevant lockkeepers. Lockkeepers must be in attendance for passage through Locks 1 - 12.

Locks

Lock No.	Rise/Fall	Lockkeeper Contact Number
Ringsend Sea Locks		Dock Superintendent +353 (0)87 258 4713
CIRCULAR LINE – LOCKS C1 TO C7		
C1 - Maquay Bridge	0.73m rise	+353 (0)86 380 5657
C2 - Lower Mount Street	2.86m rise	+353 (0)86 380 5657
C3 - Upper Mount Street	2.87m rise	+353 (0)86 380 5657
C4 - Baggot Street	2.60m rise	+353 (0)86 380 5657
C5 - Leeson Street	2.68m rise	+353 (0)86 380 5657
C6 - Charlemont Street	2.92m rise	+353 (0)86 380 5657
C7 – Portobello	2.63m rise	+353 (0)86 380 5657
MAIN LINE – LOCKS 1 TO 36		
1 (Double)	4.23m rise	+353 (0)86 827 8025
2	4.00m rise	+353 (0)86 827 8025
3 (Double)	5.97m rise	+353 (0)86 827 8025
4	3.93m rise	+353 (0)86 827 8025
5	3.11 m rise	+353 (0)86 827 8025
6	3.31m rise	+353 (0)86 827 8025
7	3.68m rise	+353 (0)87 268 3723
8	2.70m rise	+353 (0)87 268 3723
9 (Double)	4.57m rise	+353 (0)87 268 3723
10	3.15m rise	+353 (0)87 268 3723
11	3.16m rise	+353 (0)87 268 3723
12	3.58m rise	+353 (0)86 827 8025
13 (Double)	5.11m rise	+353 (0)86 827 8025
14	1.96m rise	+353 (0)87 289 5611
15	2.61m rise	+353 (0)87 289 5611
16	2.59m rise	+353 (0)87 289 5611
17	2.75m rise	+353 (0)87 289 5611
18	1.38m rise	+353 (0)87 289 5611
19 (Main Line)	2.41m fall	+353 (0)87 245 6531
20	2.65m fall	+353 (0)87 245 6537
21	2.68m fall	+353 (0)87 245 6525
22	2.65m fall	+353 (0)87 245 6525
23	2.87m fall	+353 (0)87 245 6525
24	2.99m fall	+353 (0)87 245 6525 or +353 (0)87 245 6549
25	2.90m fall	+353 (0)87 245 6549
26	2.93m fall	+353 (0)87 245 6549 or +353 (0)87 245 6541
27	2.47m fall	+353 (0)87 245 6541
28	2.65m fall	+353 (0)87 245 6541 or +353 (0)87 245 6539
29	2.47m fall	+353 (0)87 245 6539
30	2.80m fall	+353 (0)87 245 6482

31	2.71m fall	+353 (0)87 245 6482
32	2.93m fall	+353 (0)87 245 6609
33 (Double)	4.85m fall	+353 (0)87 245 6609
34	2.65m fall	+353 (0)87 245 6609 or +353 (0)87 245 6587
35	1.86m fall	+353 (0)87 245 6587
36	Variable	+353 (0)87 245 6587
BARROW LINE – LOCKS 19 TO 28		
19 Old Barrow Line	2.41m fall	+353 (0)87 245 6531
20 Ballyteague	1.89m fall	+353 (0)87 951 0444
21 Ballyteague	2.13m fall	+353 (0)87 951 0444
22 Glenaree	3.05m fall	+353 (0)86 380 7534
23 (double)	5.24m fall	+353 (0)86 380 7534
24 (double)	3.90m fall	+353 (0)87 247 3093
25	2.74m fall	+353 (0)87 247 3093
26	3.43m fall	+353 (0)87 951 0777
27	2.83m fall	+353 (0)87 951 0777
28	2.59m (variable) fall	+353 (0)87 951 0777
NAAS AND CORBALLY BRANCH – LOCKS N1 TO N5		
N1	2.83m rise	+353 (0)87 289 5611
N2	2.90m rise	+353 (0)87 289 5611
N3	2.83m rise	+353 (0)87 289 5611
N4	2.80m rise	+353 (0)87 289 5611
N5	2.23m rise	+353 (0)87 289 5611

Equipment

Operation of the lock gates requires a lock-key (windlass). It is a crank about 45cm long with a handle at right angles not less than 25cm long. A 3cm square hole with sides parallel to the handle will fit all rack spindles.
Lock-keys can be purchased from Waterways Ireland Eastern Regional Office, Waterways Ireland Tullamore Office, the Dock Superintendent at Ringsend, or the Lockkeepers at Lowtown, Shannon Harbour and Monasterevin (Barrow Line).

Movement through Locks
(See diagram for explanation of lock features)

Movement through locks requires the lock chamber to be filled or emptied by opening or closing gates and raising or lowering the sluices within those gates. This equalises the water level between the canal high level and canal low level. The lock-key operates the sluices via a rack and pinion system.

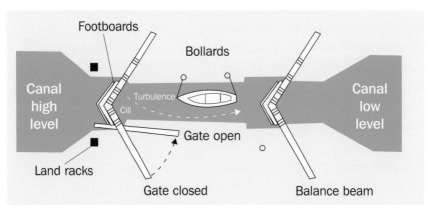

There are a number of different scenarios, depending on the direction of travel and on the position of the upper (breast) lock gates and the lower (tail) lock gates.

i) **Ascending when the lock chamber is empty**

When the lock chamber is empty, the lower gates will be open. With lower gates fully open, move boat into lock and ensure that the boat is well secured bow and stern using ropes and bollards, with crew ready to shorten the lines as the boat rises. Do not restrict the ability of the boat to move with the rising water. Close lower gates ensuring that the mitred edges meet cleanly and then close all lower sluices. It is best to raise the land tunnel racks first (if any) or the rack on the same side as the boat is tied, so that the surge of water does not tend to push the boat from the wall. Open upper sluice gently, a little at a time. Some turbulence will be generated when the first upper gate rack is raised so ropes should be tensioned or restrained, but not tied. The boat will tend to surge forward. Only when the turbulence eases off should a second rack be opened. Crew should also take care that no part of the boat is caught under any projection. When water equalises, open upper gates and proceed.

ii) **Ascending when the lock chamber is full**

If the lock chamber is full, the lower gates and sluices will be closed. Close the upper gates ensuring that the mitred edges meet cleanly and then close all upper sluices. Open lower sluices. Open lower gates only when water equalises (not before) and move boat into the lock chamber. Undertake step (i) as detailed above.

iii) **Descending when the lock chamber is full**

If the lock chamber is full, the lower gates and sluices will be closed. Move boat into the lock. Pass ropes around bollards, without tying them. Ropes should be fed through during the descent, allowing the boat to move with the falling water. Ensure that ropes are free of knots and tangles and that they don't become caught in gaps between the stones on top of the lock wall.

It is good practice to always have a sharp knife or other cutting tool ready to hand, in case ropes need to be cut in an emergency. Ensure that no part of the boat can catch on any projection as it falls. Particularly keep the rudder clear of the upper gates and of the cill under them. Close the upper gates ensuring that the mitred edges meet cleanly and then close all upper sluices. Open the lower sluices. When water equalises, open the lower gates and proceed.

iv) **Descending when the lock chamber is empty**
If the lock chamber is empty, upper gates and sluices will be closed. Close the lower gates ensuring that the mitred edges meet cleanly and then close all lower sluices. Open upper sluices. When water equalises, open upper gates and move boat into the lock. Undertake step (iii) as detailed above.

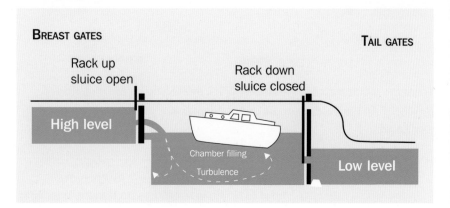

Sluice Operation

When raising sluices using the lock-key, the pawl (safety catch) will automatically move from tooth to tooth on the rack and should not be released at any time during the lift. When lowering sluices the pawl must be disengaged from the rack teeth by taking the weight of the sluice through raising the rack slightly to release the pawl. The control of the sluice is now maintained through the lock-key and great caution should be exercised in lowering the sluice. At no stage should the sluice be allowed to lower or drop by releasing the lock-key. In the final lowered position, re-engage the pawl.

Caution

DO NOT allow the sluice mechanism to lower under gravity, i.e. to simply drop without retaining control of the lock key. To do so may cause injury to person(s) or damage to the lock mechanism.

If in doubt, contact Waterways Ireland for assistance. Operating a lock requires a certain amount of physical effort; please ensure that you are sufficiently fit to do so. On no account should children (i.e. under the age of 16) be allowed to become involved in any of the lifting or lowering operations required during lock passage. Beware of staying too close to the upper cill when descending.

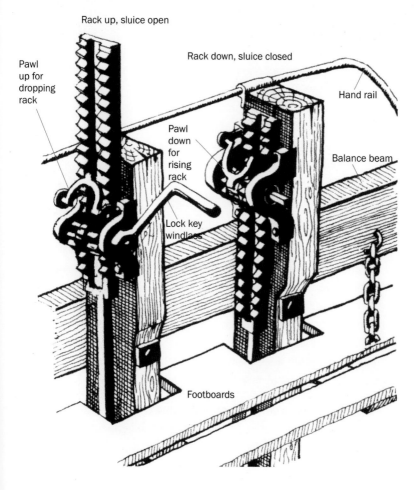

Rack up, sluice open

Rack down, sluice closed

Pawl up for dropping rack

Hand rail

Pawl down for rising rack

Balance beam

Lock key windlass

Footboards

Leaving Lock

The general rule is that unless another boat is about to use the lock, it is usual to leave the lock as it was, with the racks as you found them (i.e. if you found the lock full, leave it full).

Difficulties

Gates may jam with rubbish under them or fail to open completely due to rubbish lodging behind them. Re-opening or closing may help.

Man Overboard

Drop all racks at once and make the rescue from the boat. There are no ladders in the lock chambers.

Courtesy

While 'first come first served' is the rule, it is preferable, in order to conserve water, to give priority to a boat coming down when the lock is full or to a boat ascending when the lock is empty. Enter / leave the lock slowly, using the minimum power necessary, in order to avoid washing debris back onto the steps beneath the gates, which can prevent gates closing properly.

ANGLING ON THE GRAND CANAL

Inland Fisheries Ireland (IFI) is the state agency responsible for the protection, management and conservation of Ireland's inland fisheries and sea angling resources. IFI is commissioned by Waterways Ireland to conduct scientific research aimed at understanding and improving habitat conditions for fish and aquatic life on the Royal Canal, Grand Canal (Main Line & Barrow Line), the Barrow Navigation and the Shannon-Erne Waterway. Allied to this research role, close attention is focused on the requirements of anglers and other waterways users. The overall aim of the work is to enhance amenity use whilst protecting the ecological integrity of the canal network.

The Grand Canal averages 15m wide and is approximately 1.75m deep, although deeper water is available at certain locations. Canal water can be very clear, which can make day-time fishing difficult. Accordingly, angling is often most productive towards dawn and dusk. The canal corridor supports a wide diversity of aquatic and riparian plants that harbour myriads of fish-food insects. The vegetation is carefully managed and does not pose an obstruction for anglers. Whilst most species are widespread throughout the canal, bream are particularly abundant in the westerly reaches. Tench, meanwhile, are especially common in the canal east of the summit at Lowtown.

No licence or permit is required to fish on the Grand Canal, and the fishery is open all year. Up to date fisheries regulations are available from the IFI website **www.fishinginireland.info/regulations.htm**

Angling Centres of Excellence

IFI and Fáilte Ireland are jointly working towards delivering a strategy to develop Irish angling tourism, in recognition of the important economic contribution made by angling. Part of the delivery of this strategy involves the setting and publishing of standards for those providing products and services to anglers – standards which are clearly based on customer (not supplier) expectations and needs. The identification of 'Centres of Excellence', where anglers can experience the best of fishing, accommodation, food and support services/activities, will start the process of encouraging the industry to provide high quality angling experiences in Ireland. Examples of such Centres of Excellence can be found at Prosperous and Edenderry.

Fishing Tackle and Bait

For most fish species, pole or float is the method of choice. At the beginning of a session, anglers should firstly target the middle, fishing the bait just on the bottom. Try introducing a small amount of groundbait at the start of the session (between four and eight small balls) and loose feed thereafter. It may be worth adding some extra groundbait if a number of cruisers pass. Careful pre-baiting can work for anglers targeting larger species. Fish with no. 6 or 8 elastic, 1.4kg main line to a 0.9kg hook length, and a medium-wire, size 18 hook. As a general rule the lighter the tackle the greater the catch. However, large fish patrol the canal, and, if hooked, will test your equipment, so be prepared to introduce heavier terminal tackle. A wide range of hook baits work, although white and red maggot, pinkies, casters and worm often work best. It is worth having corn on standby, particularly if larger species are targeted.

Good pike fishing is available throughout the canal, particularly where shoals of large fodder fish, such as bream and hybrids, reside. A roving approach, continuously covering new water, should maximise sport. A wide range of techniques will work including dead-baits or artificial lures. Fly fishing for pike can also be productive, and the canal is ideally suited to this method. Basic pike tackle incorporating suitable wire trace should be employed whatever method is used.

Roach are the most numerous fish species present throughout the Grand Canal, normally representing in excess of 70% of fish numbers. While roach are relative newcomers to many Irish canal fisheries  they are now ubiquitous and form the basis of many match and pleasure fisheries. Roach can reach a maximum size of 2kg and typically average between 50 to 100g in weight. Good numbers of larger fish can be found along the canal. Roach are easily identified by their bright silver colouration and their orange-red fins and eyes.

Baits: Maggots, casters, bread, paste, sweetcorn, worms.
Specimen Weight: 0.907kg; Irish Record: 1.425kg

Bream are traditionally one of the favourite fish species for coarse anglers. A shoal fish, they can reach a maximum size of 7kg. In the canal, adult bream typically average 1-2kg. Anglers targeting  canal bream search for the areas of coloured water that signal the presence of feeding bream shoals. Adult bream are recognized by their bronze colour, black fins and protruding upper jaw. Young bream or 'skimmers' differ from adults due to their silver colouring.

Baits: Maggots, worms, casters, sweetcorn, bread, paste.
Specimen Weight: 3.402kg; Irish Record: 5.528kg

Roach x bream hybrids occur wherever the parent species coexist, but can also be found in the absence of bream. A hard fighting fish, they are a popular angling quarry. Intermediate in appearance  between the parent species, large hybrids can be distinguished from bream by their shorter anal fin. Hybrids can weigh up to 4kg, but a fish over 0.5kg would be regarded as a good canal catch.

Baits: Maggots, worms, casters, sweetcorn, bread, paste.
Specimen Weight: 1.6kg; Irish Record: 3.175kg

Tench are an increasingly popular angling quarry and are widespread throughout the canal network, but are particularly abundant east of the summit level at Lowtown. Tell-tale fizzy bubbles on the surface of  the water betray the presence of feeding tench to observant anglers. While tench can weigh up to 5kg, the typical fish will weigh around 1 to 2kg. An attractive fish, tench are a dark olive or blackish colour with rounded fins and an almost unforked tail. They have distinctive, bright red eyes.

Baits: Maggots, casters, sweetcorn, bread, paste, worms, mini boilies.
Specimen Weight: 2.721kg; Irish Record: 3.697kg

Rudd are widespread but present in relatively low numbers, having been largely out-competed by the closely related roach. While the rudd can attain a maximum size of 2.5kg, they typically average 50  to 100g in weight. Rudd can be distinguished from roach by their more golden, rounded appearance. The fins of rudd are a vivid, bright red colour. They have a pronounced, protruding lower jaw which allows them to feed on the surface of the canal.

Baits: Maggots, bread, casters, sweetcorn, paste, worms, flies.
Specimen Weight: 0.9kg; Irish Record: 2.041kg

Perch can be found throughout the canal. Reaching a maximum size of 3kg (typically much smaller on the canal), perch are aggressive, greedy feeders. They are rough and prickly  to the touch and are easily recognised by the characteristic vertical dark stripes along their usually green flanks. Perch have two dorsal fins, the first of which is well armed with very sharp spines.

Baits: Worms, maggots, casters, small dead fish and a range of spinning baits.
Specimen Weight: 1.2kg; Irish Record: 2.646kg

Pike are ubiquitous throughout the Grand Canal. In exceptional circumstances pike weigh up to 20kg and can grow up to 1.3m in length. While they typically average 2 to  3kg in weight, specimens in excess of 10kg are present. Pike are fish eaters and are perfectly designed to do so. The pike has a streamlined, torpedo shaped body, and its mottled olive green colour provides perfect camouflage. It has a cavernous mouth with rows of needle sharp, backward pointing teeth.

Baits: Range of deadbaits, spinners and plugs including jerkbaits and flies.
Specimen Weight: Lake: 13.608kg, River: 9.072kg;
Irish Record: Lake: 19.391kg, River: 19.051kg

Carp A 'specialists' fish that are relatively uncommon on most canal sections. They can be fished for in certain isolated locations, although they can be difficult to catch. Carp are renowned  as one of the hardest fighting freshwater fish. Reaching a maximum size of 14kg, canal carp up to 10kg have been reported. Fish of 4 to 5kg would be typical. Two varieties of carp are found in the Grand Canal. These are the fully scaled common and the partially scaled mirror carp. Dull brown in colour, carp are a stocky muscular fish, with an elongated dorsal fin. Four barbels on the large mouth help the carp detect food items on the canal bottom.

Baits: Maggots, casters, boilies, sweetcorn, worms, bread, fishnuts
Specimen Weight: 5.443kg; Irish Record: 13.523kg

Waterways Ireland advocates a **Catch and Release** Policy on all of it's waterways

CYCLING THE GRAND CANAL

In general, canal towpaths are not suitable for cycling due to their surfacing and the potential for damage to be caused to the natural environment. However, specific sections of the towpath of the Grand Canal have been upgraded to ensure the safety of all users of the towpath section of the cycle route. Waterways Ireland will continue to participate in discussions regarding the Government's sustainable "Smarter Travel" transport policy and in particular the *"National Cycle Policy Framework 2009 – 2020"* as it relates to the canal.

Green Route

In June 2010 the Green Route, a high quality pedestrian and cycle path was officially opened. A distance of 8.5km, the route extends from the 3rd Lock in Inchicore to the 12th Lock in Lucan. The Green Route project was initiated by South Dublin County Council, Dublin City Council, ESB Networks and Waterways Ireland. The scheme opened up one of the country's most scenic waterways to the public by providing easy access and security along the route, employing the latest technology in CCTV and public lighting. The scheme included extensive tree and shrub planting which enhances habitats for flora and fauna along the route.

Premium Cycle Route

In March 2012, the Premium Cycle Route from Portobello to Sherriff Street along the Grand Canal officially opened. The 3.5km route passes Lesson St Bridge, Dublin's Docklands and the Samuel Beckett Bridge. This route is an ideal opportunity for families, young people and visitors to get around Dublin.

WALKING THE GRAND CANAL

National Waymarked Ways

National Waymarked Ways have been designed to cater for walkers of all ages, of reasonable health and fitness, and are planned so that, in the right conditions, anyone should be able to walk any of them, at their own pace. Comprehensive waymarking consisting of frequent signposts with a motif of a walking figure and an arrow in bright yellow indicating the way, means that there are no direction-finding challenges on Ireland's waymarked trails. Walkers should be aware, however, that in some places a waymark sign may be missing or hidden by summer foliage, so on occasions some map-reading may be required to ensure arrival at the intended destination.

For comfort and safety, and to enable you to enjoy your walk on a waymarked trail fully, the following recommendations should be adopted:

- Wear sturdy and comfortable shoes that give your ankles support and for at least most of the day, keep your feet dry.

- Carry a rucksack with waterproof gear in case of rain, and additional warm clothing in case of cold. It is also important to carry adequate water and an energy-giving snack or picnic.

- Study a map and/or a guide when you are planning to walk the route, and bring them with you.

- Never walk alone in isolated areas, and always let someone know where you are going and when you should be expected back.

- Always show respect for the countryside and for the people who live and work in it and follow the guiding principles of "Leave No Trace" www.leavenotraceireland.org

The Grand Canal Way

The Grand Canal was designed to connect Dublin, Ireland's capital city westwards through the midlands with the River Shannon and, although construction work began in 1757, the waterway was not completed as far as the Shannon until 1804. It closed to commercial traffic in 1951, but in recent decades the canal has been restored for amenity use, and is well frequented by pleasure craft of all kinds. The Grand Canal Way follows pleasant grassy towpaths, gravel and sometimes tarmac canal-side roads from Dublin to Shannon Harbour, where the canal meets with Ireland's longest river. The route is an informal linear park punctuated by the locks that characterise canal technology, carefully restored surviving lockkeepers cottages, and the towns and villages whose existence is owed to the trade and commerce the canal brought in the 18th and 19th centuries. Much of the landscape through which the route passes has been untouched by modern agriculture and remains a linear oasis for the flora and fauna that was originally common throughout our countryside. The many towns and villages along the way provide walkers with accommodation possibilities along the route, and as public transport options are good, these places can act as starting and finishing points for those who want to sample only sections of the route. Dogs, under effective control are allowed; please clean up after your dog.

The Offaly Way

The Offaly Way is a 29km linear walking route in the midlands of Ireland that links the Slieve Bloom Way at the old village of Cadamstown with the Grand Canal Way and ends a few kilometres north of the canal at the ancient monastic site of Lemanaghan. This short route takes in a rich collection of features that will ensure many walkers will want to linger along the way, including the scenic Silver River; an old bridge that Red Hugh O'Donnell's army is said to have crossed en route to the Battle of Kinsale in 1601; a rare Mesolithic site at Boora; St Manchan's holy well; and St Mella's Cell, a tiny early Christian church at Lemanaghan. The terrain consists of mainly quiet side roads and a couple of riverbank paths that are often wet and muddy in places. There is a shortage of overnight accommodation in the area, but Cadamstown is served by public transport. There are two or three loop walks in Boora Parkland including one which is wheelchair friendly. In this area there are a number of recreational projects and amenities, and experiments are being carried out on how to best use the landscape that has been stripped of its peat. 17kms or 46% of the Way follows local roads. Keep dogs under close control. For full details and maps of the various sections of the the Grand Canal Way and the Offaly Way visit **www.irishtrails.ie**

Slí na Sláinte

Slí na Sláinte stands for 'path to health'. Developed by the Irish Heart Foundation - the national heart and stroke charity - it's the outgoing way to make walking far more enjoyable. You'll find Slí na Sláinte walking routes all over Ireland. They are marked by bright colourful signposts which are not numbered and are situated at 1km intervals. Simply follow the km signs, set your pace to suit your enjoyment.

Slí na Sláinte Routes

Tullamore Slí - The Tullamore Slí is a 5.4km route which starts at the Kilbeggan Bridge on the Grand Canal. To follow the route, continue out the Kilbeggan road past O'Connor Park and the Hospital on your right. Just after the first kilometre pole at the roundabout, turn left down Collins Lane. Continue along this road passing the next kilometre pole, and go straight through the Clara road roundabout.

Slí na Sláinte

At the Rahan roundabout, continue left past the 3rd kilometre post, keeping IDA Srah Business Park on your left onto Rahan road. At the next roundabout at the entrance to the Srah Business Park continue straight heading for the Clara Bridge on the canal. Cross Clara road and continue straight onto Clontarf road back to the starting point on the Kilbeggan Bridge.

Cloghan K Slí - The Cloghan K Slí route is a 1km route which starts at St Rynagh's Football GAA Club on the Birr road. The route circuits the playing pitch and continues onto Hill Street via the Old Mass Path. The route is completed by turning back onto Banagher Street and then back to the starting point. The pathway is suitable for wheelchair users and has full lighting. The route has been developed in partnership between St Rynagh's Football GAA Club and the Cloghan Development Association with funding from Offaly Local Development Company, West Offaly Enterprise Fund (ESB), Leinster Council (GAA) and the HSE.

CANOEING & ROWING ON THE GRAND CANAL

The still waters of the Grand Canal provide a beautiful and tranquil environment in which to enjoy canoeing and rowing. Access can be gained via slipways and these are indicated on the individual maps contained in this guide. It is also possible to access at some jetties where the freeboard is low enough, and at some quay walls, again dependent on suitable water levels.

Canoeing

Canoeing is the collective term used to describe a wide-ranging and multifaceted activity that encompasses competitive and non-competitive forms of canoeing and kayaking. Non-competitive canoeing includes the less formalised types of kayaking and canoeing activities that are mainly based on journeying and adventuring, while within competitive canoeing, there are opportunities to take part in numerous specialised disciplines such as Canoe Slalom, Marathon Racing, Flat Water Racing, Freestyle and Canoe Polo.

Many indigenous peoples have developed "canoe" crafts. The modern "Canadian Canoe" derives from a canoe form evolved by the native North American Indians, who used native birch bark to fashion a light, versatile craft. Modern open canoes, now used mainly for recreational touring, employ modern materials but their shape remains virtually unchanged from the age-old designs of their ancestors. Other forms of canoes have been developed, mainly for specialised use in competition but regardless of shape, a craft is identified as a canoe if the occupant or occupants would normally kneel and use a single-bladed paddle.

The open canoe is a relatively stable and immensely versatile craft which is normally paddled by two people but can be handled solo. To learn to paddle a canoe as a doubles pair requires effective communication and the development of good teamwork between partners. It is perhaps these characteristics which represent part of its worth as an educational medium.

Kayaking as a recreational activity provides opportunities for adventure, relaxation, exploration, and competition. The challenge of descending a white-water river or gracefully meandering quiet lakes and canals are all part of kayaking's special appeal. Kayaks are frequently used for expeditions at sea and represent the ideal craft for close investigation of Ireland's spectacular coastlines.

Kayaking has long been recognised as a useful medium for outdoor education and is of particular value in building confidence, self-reliance and co-operation. Kayaks come in many different forms but whatever its shape and appearance, the features which identify a craft as a kayak are that the occupant or occupants sit and use a double-bladed paddle.

Canoeing is an adventure sport and participants are strongly recommended to seek the advice of the sport's governing body, Canoeing Ireland, before venturing onto the navigation. Canoeists are reminded of the inherent danger associated with operating close to weirs and locks, particularly when rivers are in flood and large volumes of water are moving through the navigation due to general flood conditions. Portage is required at all locks (carrying canoe around the lock, rather than travelling through it) however a heavily laden canoe may be put through a lock unmanned, provided it is attended with a head and stern line. Further details can be found on **www.canoe.ie**

Rowing

The sport of rowing has evolved over centuries from a means of propelling warships, to a popular hobby and spectator sport. In Ireland there are over 5,000 people involved in the sport of rowing, from competitive oars-people to coaches and umpires.

The fine boat, also known as the Olympic class boat, is the racing shell – it generally has one, two, four or eight seats. The eights will always have a coxswain (cox) to steer and direct the crew, whereas a four may be coxed or coxless depending on the type of boat used. In 'sweep' boats, each rower has one oar (or blade). In 'sculling' boats, the oarsmen use two blades.

Touring rowing boats are a wider version of the shape than those used for competitive rowing. Tours are a fun and sociable way to row but they can also be endurance events that require stamina and aerobic fitness - a great way to keep fit. Recreational rowing can be enjoyed by all the family, not only keeping rowers in the sport but also recruiting new people, young and old, ensuring continuing generations of active members. Rowing Ireland is the Governing Body for Rowing in Ireland and represents over 80 clubs across the four provinces. Further details can be found on **www.iaru.ie**

Canoeing and Rowing Clubs

Joining a club provides excellent opportunities to take part in canoeing and rowing activities and learn from more experienced members. The club scene in Ireland is extremely social and a great way to meet new people as you explore these sports.

Celbridge Paddlers Canoe Club

Email: cpaddlers@hotmail.com
Celbridge Paddlers Canoe Club is situated at Aylmer's Bridge on the Grand Canal about two miles south west of Celbridge town in County Kildare. Current membership stands at roughly 120 and is drawn mainly from the Celbridge and surrounding area. The Club is very much a part of the local community with close links to local schools. Celbridge Paddlers is traditionally a marathon racing club has been very successful both at home and abroad at marathon and sprint events. In more recent times it has become involved in other canoeing

disciplines such as Canoe Polo, Freestyle (Rodeo) and Wild Water racing. The canal provides a safe environment for beginners and also provides an ideal flat-water training location for serious marathon and sprint squad sessions.

Tullamore Canoe Club

Email: tuccmail@gmail.com
Tel: +353 (0)86 825 8319
Tullamore Canoe Club is a training centre that provides high standard water sports training with a high emphasis on safety and fun to the Tullamore community. The club aims to provide a safe learning environment to improve and develop skills and co-ordination, physical health, awareness of nature and Ireland's vast wealth of navigable waterways, to provide access to equipment and training and to promote the sport of canoeing.

Offaly Rowing Club

Email: info@offalyrowing.ie
Offaly Rowing Club is affiliated to the Irish Amateur Rowing Union and was established in 1985. The club is located at Lock 23 on the Grand Canal outside Tullamore, Co Offaly. Offaly Rowing Club has been providing access to rowing for people with disabilities through the adaptive rowing boat programme at the club house. Offaly Rowing Club also participates in the new indoor rowing programme using ergometers in association with secondary schools throughout the county.

WILDLIFE ON THE GRAND CANAL

The Grand Canal is a man-made waterway that was originally constructed to cater for commercial traffic. It is now an important wildlife corridor stretching from Dublin City to the Shannon at Shannon Harbour. Its ecological significance is recognised through its designation as a proposed Natural Heritage Area under the Wildlife Act (Site Code: 002104). In addition the Grand Canal is designated as an artificial waterbody under the Water Framework Directive and as such is required to meet the standard of Good Ecological Potential (GEP), which it currently does.

The ecological value of the canal lies more in the number of species it supports along its linear habitats, than in the presence of rare species, although a number of rare species are found. Such rare and protected species include freshwater crayfish, lamprey, opposite leaved pondweed and kingfisher to name but a few.

A diverse range of aquatic plants occur within the canals. These include Hornworts, Pondweeds, Arrowhead and Crowfoot. In the riparian zone, plants such as Branched Bur-reed, Common Club Rush, Reed Sweet Grass and Yellow Iris are commonly found. This diversity of plants ensures a wide range of insects and higher animals such as fish and mammals will also be found. The reed fringe acts as a buffer to disperse wave energy and therefore is excellent for bank protection.

The habitats to be found immediately along the canal include open water, riparian fringe, towpath, calcareous grassland, scrub, trees and hedgerows and in some areas fen and wetland habitat. This habitat diversity in turn lends itself to a diverse range of insects, plants and animals. Unlike natural systems, management of the canal corridor is essential to maintain both its navigation function but also its ecological value.

The hedgerows and treelines along the canal system are hugely important, acting as wildlife corridors and refuges, with over half of all bird species in Ireland using them for nesting and breeding. Birds found along the navigation include Heron, Coot, Moorhen and Mallard, as well as EU protected species such as Kingfisher, and songbirds such as Blackbirds and Robins. Hundreds of different species of invertebrates can be found in hedgerows from the leaves to the twigs to the bark and roots. Bats also like to roost in old, hollow hedgerow trees and hunt for insects along the hedge itself, as well as using their linear structure when using echolocation to traverse the landscape. In particular, species such as Daubenton's Bat specifically use the canal when foraging, flying close to the water's surface and snatching insects mid flight.

© Edward W Delaney

Many of Ireland's mammals use the canal as wildlife corridors for burrows and feeding sites. Mammals found along and within the hedges include Fox, Badger, Field Mouse and Pygmy Shrew. The Grand Canal is also very important for Otters. Next time you are on your boat or walking along the Grand Canal Way keep an eye out for these elusive graceful creatures. More often than not they will hear you and scamper away long before you see them. However the keen eye will pick up otter activity such as slides (a noticeable area of flattened grass/sediment where otters gain access to the water) or couches (prominent resting areas where faeces may also be visible). Otters have also been spotted in heavily urbanised areas such as the Grand Canal Basin in Dublin's city centre.

Invasive species are unfortunately also present along the navigation. Waterways Ireland would urge boaters to be very careful to ensure these

species are not spread. Of particular concern along the Grand Canal is Japanese Knotweed, though other species such as Nuttall's Pondweed, New Zealand Pygmyweed, Giant Hogweed and Zebra Mussel are also present. Further information on invasive species along the Grand Canal can be found at www.caisie.ie www.invasivespeciesireland.com or www.fisheriesireland.ie

ATTRACTIONS ALONG THE GRAND CANAL

There are many and varied attractions to be enjoyed along the length of the Grand Canal, particularly in and around metropolitan Dublin. What follows is not intended as a comprehensive travel guide but it will give a flavour of the diversity and quality of those attractions which are most accessible from the Grand Canal. You should make contact by telephone, or access the relevant website for further information including opening times. Public facilities are also listed; Libraries, Playgrounds and Swimming Pools.

For further details or information about other attractions, you should contact Fáilte Ireland Dublin on +353 (0)1 884 7700, or Fáilte Ireland East/Lakelands on +353 (0)44 9344 000 or visit www.discoverireland.ie

Waterways Ireland Visitor Centre
Grand Canal Quay, Dublin 2

Web: www.waterwaysirelandvisitorcentre.org

Tel: +353 (0)1 677 7510

Description: Affectionately known as The Box in the Docks, the centre is a family friendly visitor attraction located on the waters of Grand Canal Dock.

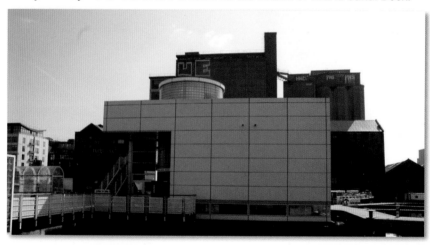

Jeanie Johnston
Custom House Quay, Dublin 1

Web: www.jeaniejohnston.ie

Tel: +353 (0)1 473 0111

Description: A step aboard the Jeanie Johnston is a step towards understanding the daunting experience of the millions of people who crossed the Atlantic, a 3,000 mile voyage, braving gales and harsh seas, seeking survival and hope in the new world of North America. A tour of the re-created Jeanie Johnston enables visitors to see what it was like on board a wooden, tall ship during the famine era. The tour will convey a deep sense of history and will be a memorable experience for all who come on board.

Bord Gáis Energy Theatre
Grand Canal Quay, Dublin 2

Web: www.bordgaisenergytheatre.ie

Tel: +353 (0)1 677 7999

Description: Opened in March 2010, the Bord Gáis Energy Theatre offers a diverse programme of theatrical experiences to meet everyone's passion and interests including ballets, musicals, family shows, drama, concerts, comedy, orchestral and opera.

Old Jameson Distillery
Bow St, Smithfield Village, Dublin 7

Web: www.tours.jamesonwhiskey.com

Tel: +353 (0)1 807 2355

Description: Open seven days a week, a visit to the Old Jameson Distillery is an unforgettable experience. Take a tour and sample the taste of some of Ireland's finest Irish Whiskey.

Guinness Storehouse
St James's Gate, Dublin 8

Web: www.guinness-storehouse.com

Tel: +353 (0)1 408 4800

Description: Ireland's number one visitor attraction, this historic building is central to Dublin's and Ireland's heritage and has been continually updated to create a blend of fascinating industrial tradition with a contemporary edge.

National Museum of Ireland
Collins Barracks, Benburb Street, Dublin 7

Web: www.museum.ie

Tel: +353 (0)1 677 7444

Description: Originally an army barracks, the museum is now home to a wide range of Decorative Arts and History, which include weaponry, furniture, silver, jewellery, ceramics and glassware, as well as examples of folk life and costume.

Dublinia
St. Michael's Hill, Christchurch, Dublin 8

Web: www.dublinia.ie

Tel: +353 (0)1 679 4611

Description: Lose yourself in Viking & Medieval Dublin. Dublinia is an unforgettable experience in a historically important location at the heart of Dublin City, the crossroads where modern and old Dublin meet.

Castletown House
Celbridge, Co Kildare

Web: www.castletown.ie

Tel: +353 (0)1 628 8252

Description: Access to the house is by guided tour only. The tour covers all aspects of the history of Castletown House, from 1722, when it was built, right up to the present day and the recent work which has been undertaken. The diverse and fascinating Connolly family members who lived in the house are explained, and visitors get a chance to view the fine architecture, original furniture and vast collection of paintings within Castletown.

Tullamore Dew Visitor Centre
Bury Quay, Tullamore, Co Offaly

Web: www.tullamoredewvisitorcentre.com

Tel: +353 (0)57 932 5015

Description: Discover Tullamore Dew's distinctive character from its spiritual home in Tullamore, deep in Ireland's heart.

Lough Boora Parklands
Teach Lea, Leabeg, Tullamore, Co Offaly

Web: www.loughbooraparklands.com

Tel: +353 (0)57 934 5978

Description: The Lough Boora Parklands development consists of a magnificent collection of natural & manmade lakes, wetlands, woodland areas, 50km of walkways, natural recolonisation and pastureland, which has provided a new habitat for wildlife, flora & fauna. It comprises four distinct areas: Lough Boora Parklands, Turraun Wetlands, Finnamore's Lakes area and Cloghan Wetlands/Loch Clochan. The Parklands can be enjoyed throughout the four seasons. There are information signs at the car-parks that give details relating to the site histories and also about the flora & fauna. The extensive wetlands now attract wintering flocks of wildfowl. The 50km of paths range in length from a short stroll to 5km on a level landscape which can be enjoyed by all age groups. Whether taking a closer look at the Parkland's flora and fauna, or simply taking a quiet walk or bike ride, these paths are the ideal way to see the Parklands.

Clara Bog Nature Reserve
Clara to Rahan Road, Clara, Co Offaly

Web: www.npws.ie

Tel: +353 (0)57 936 8878

Description: Clara Bog is designated as a Special Area of Conservation (SAC) and a statutory Nature Reserve, established in 1987. It covers approximately 460 hectares, and is situated about 2km south-east of Clara town. The Visitor Centre for Clara Bog is co-located at the library in Clara.

Playgrounds, Pools and Libraries

Playgrounds

Ringsend Park, Ringsend, Dublin 4

South Dock Street Park, Dublin 4

Belgrave Square Park, Rathmines, Dublin 6

Harold's Cross Park, Harold's Cross, Dublin 6

Jim Mitchell Park, Ring Street, Inchicore, Dublin 8

Cherry Orchard Park, Ballyfermot, Dublin 10

Markievicz Park, Ballyfermot, Dublin 10

Corkagh Park Playground, Clondalkin, Dublin 22

Edenderry Playground, Edenderry, Co Offaly

Lloyd Town Park, Tullamore, Co Offaly

Shannon Harbour, Co Offaly

Riverbank, Monasterevin, Co Kildare

Athy Public Playground, Church Road, Athy, Co Kildare

Swimming Pools

Crumlin Swimming Pool, Pearse Park, Windmill Road, Crumlin, Dublin 12
Tel: +353 (0)1 455 5792

Markievicz Leisure Centre, Townsend Street, Dublin 2
Tel: +353 (0)1 222 6130
Email: markievicz.leisurecentre@dublincity.ie

Ballyfermot Leisure Centre, Blackditch Road, Ballyfermot, Dublin 10
Tel: +353 (0)1 222 8580
Email: ballyfermot.lc@dublincity.ie

Clondalkin Leisure Centre, Nangor Road, Clondalkin, Dublin 22
Tel: +353 (0)1 457 4858
Email: info@clondalkinleisure.com

Edenderry Swimming Pool, St Conlaith's Road, Edenderry, Co Offaly
Tel: +353 (0)46 973 1294
Email: swim@edenderryswimmingpool.ie

Tullamore Leisure Centre, Hophill Road, Tullamore, Co Offaly
Tel: +353 (0)57 932 9398
Email: information@auragroup.ie

Libraries

Ringsend Library
Fitzwilliam Street, Dublin 4
Tel: +353 (0)1 668 0063
Email: ringsendlibrary@dublincity.ie

Pearse Street Library
138-144 Pearse Street, Dublin 2
Tel: +353 (0)1 674 4888
Email: pearsestreetlibrary@dublincity.ie

Kevin Street Library
18 Lower Kevin Street, Dublin 2
Tel: +353 (0)1 475 3794
Email: kevinstreetlibrary@dublincity.ie

Rathmines Library
157 Lower Rathmines Road, Dublin 6
Tel: +353 (0)1 497 3539
Email: rathmineslibrary@dublincity.ie

Dolphin's Barn Library
Parnell Road, Dublin 12
Tel: +353 (0)1 454 0681
Email: dolphinsbarnlibrary@dublincity.ie

Inchicore Library
34 Emmet Road, Dublin 8
Tel: +353 (0)1 453 3793
Email: inchicorelibrary@dublincity.ie

Ballyfermot Library
Ballyfermot Road, Dublin 10
Tel: +353 (0)1 626 9324
Email: ballyfermotlibrary@dublincity.ie

Clondalkin Library
Monastery Road, Clondalkin, Dublin 22
Tel: +353 (0)1 459 3315
Email: clondalkin@sdublincoco.ie

Edenderry Library
JKL Street, Edenderry, Co Offaly
Tel: +353 (0)46 973 1028
Email: edenderrylibrary@offalycoco.ie

Daingean Library
Main Street, Daingean, Co Offaly
Tel: +353 (0)57 935 3005
Email: daingeanlibrary@offalycoco.ie

Tullamore Library
O'Connor Square, Tullamore, Co Offaly
Tel: +353 (0)57 934 6832
Email: tullamorelibrary@offalycoco.ie

Ferbane Library
Gallen, Ferbane, Co Offaly
Tel: +353 (0)90 645 4259
Email: ferbanelibrary@offalycoco.ie

Banagher Library
Moore's Corner, Banagher, Co Offaly
Tel: +353 (0)57 915 1471
Email: banagherlibrary@offalycoco.ie

Rathangan Library
Canal Court, Rathangan, Co Kildare
Tel: +353 (0)45 528 078
Email: rathanganlib@kildarecoco.ie

Monasterevin Library
Watermill Place, Monasterevin, Co Kildare
Tel: +353 (0)45 529 239
Email: monasterevinlib@kildarecoco.ie

Athy Library
Emily Square, Athy, Co Kildare
Tel: +353 (0)59 863 1144
Email: athylib@kildarecoco.ie

CHRONOLOGICAL HISTORY

1751	Establishment of the Commissioners of Inland Navigation.
1756	Work commenced on the Grand Canal Scheme.
1763	Thomas Omer, Engineer, reported three locks and ten miles of canal dug from Clondalkin westward.
1765	Dublin Corporation took over the completion of the canal to the River Morell in order to obtain a water supply.
1772	The Company of the Undertakers of the Grand Canal were incorporated.
1773	Foundation stone of 1st Lock laid by Earl Harcourt and work began on city sections.
1777	Water supply from the River Morell to the City Basin near St James's Street commenced.
1779	Canal opened to traffic to Sallins.
1780	First passage boat began to ply to Sallins.
1784	Passage boat service extended to Robertstown.
1785	Barrow Line completed to Monasterevin.
1789	Kildare Canal Company completed a branch to Naas.
1790	Work began on the Circular Line and it was completed to Portobello.
1791	Barrow Line to Athy completed.
1796	Ringsend Docks completed.
1797	Main Line completed to Daingean (Philipstown).
1798	Main Line completed to Tullamore.
1803	Canal completed to the Shannon but staunching problems delayed the opening.
1804	First trade boat passed through the canal from the Shannon.
1808	Grand Canal Company purchased the Naas Branch.
1810	Naas Branch completed to Corbally.
1824	Work began on the Ballinasloe Branch.
1827	Work began on the Mountmellick Branch.
1828	Ballinasloe Branch opened to traffic.
1830	Work began on the Kilbeggan Branch.
1831	Mountmellick Branch opened to traffic.
1834	Fast fly boats commenced.
1835	Kilbeggan Branch opened to traffic.
1852	Last of the passenger boats withdrawn.
1950	Grand Canal Company merged with Coras Iompair Eireann (CIE).

Photo courtesy: Conor Nolan

1960	CIE withdrew the trade boats.
1961	Ballinasloe, Mountmellick, Kilbeggan and Naas Branches officially closed to navigation.
1974	James's Street Harbour closed to navigation.
1986	Grand Canal system transferred to the Office of Public Works.
1987	Naas Branch re-opened to Naas Harbour.
1996	The Grand Canal system and the other inland waterways under the control of the OPW were transferred to the Waterways Service of the Department of Arts, Culture and the Gaeltacht, and became part of Dúchas, The Heritage Service of the Department of Arts, Heritage, Gaeltacht and the Islands in 1997.
1999	Waterways Ireland was established as one of the six North/South Implementation Bodies under the British Irish Agreement and has responsibility for the management, maintenance, development and restoration of specified inland navigable waterways, principally for recreational purposes.

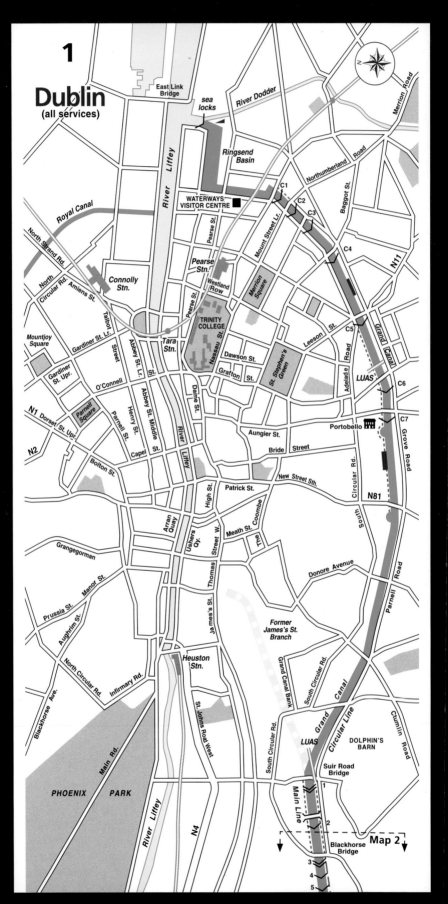

1

Dublin
(all services)

MAPS & GUIDES 1 TO 15
DUBLIN TO SHANNON HARBOUR

SECTION 1   Circular Line to Inchicore

Route Description

Entrance to the Grand Canal system is through one of the sea locks from the tidal River Liffey, near the mouth of the River Dodder. For two hours either side of low water, there is less than 0.9m over the cill but boats may tie up to the quay below the lock to wait for the tide.

Headroom under General McMahon bridge, which separates the outer from the inner Ringsend Basin is about 2.7m at normal water level. There is a 56-berth marina at the Waterways Ireland Visitor Centre, which is commonly known as "the Box in the Docks". The exit from the inner basin is under an arched railway bridge with about 2.65m headroom in the centre. Owing to the curve of the arch there is less room in practice - 2.45m over a width of 3m. It is important to keep out approximately 0.45m from the campshire on the west bank, to maximise headroom. There is a very difficult corner to negotiate before passing under Maquay Bridge. From here there are seven locks close together followed by a 3km level from Portobello to 1st Lock, Main Line. This is at the junction of the Circular Line and the old line to James Street Harbour, which has been filled in and is now used by the LUAS.

The public road and Dublin's LUAS tram lines accompany the canal all the way to Blackhorse Bridge, Inchicore. 1st Lock is double-chambered but doubles count as one in the numbering system. Some rubbish may be picked up in the urban areas by propellers, especially on deep-draught vessels and care should be taken to limit throttle to account for this.

Facilities

All Services: Dublin
Slip: Grand Canal Dock, Ringsend (contact Dock Superintendent in advance at +353 (0)87 258 4713)

History

Dublin's original canal terminus was James's Street Harbour beside the city basin, because one of the objectives of the canal builders was to provide a reliable source of drinking water. In 1790, with the canal completed to Athy, work began on the link with the Liffey. The more obvious route from James's Street was supplanted by an ambitious scheme following the recently completed Circular Road. With financial assistance from the Government, the Circular Line and Ringsend Docks were completed and a lavish opening ceremony held on 23 April 1796. Portobello Hotel was opened in 1807 and became the passage boat terminus. It ceased to operate as an hotel in the 1850s and for many years was a hospital before being converted into offices.

There is a statue of Patrick Kavanagh on a seat by the canal on the north bank above Baggot Street Bridge inspired by his poem "Lines written on a Seat on the Grand Canal, Dublin". After the annual St Patrick's day parade, a group of Kavanagh's friends gather at the seat in his honour.

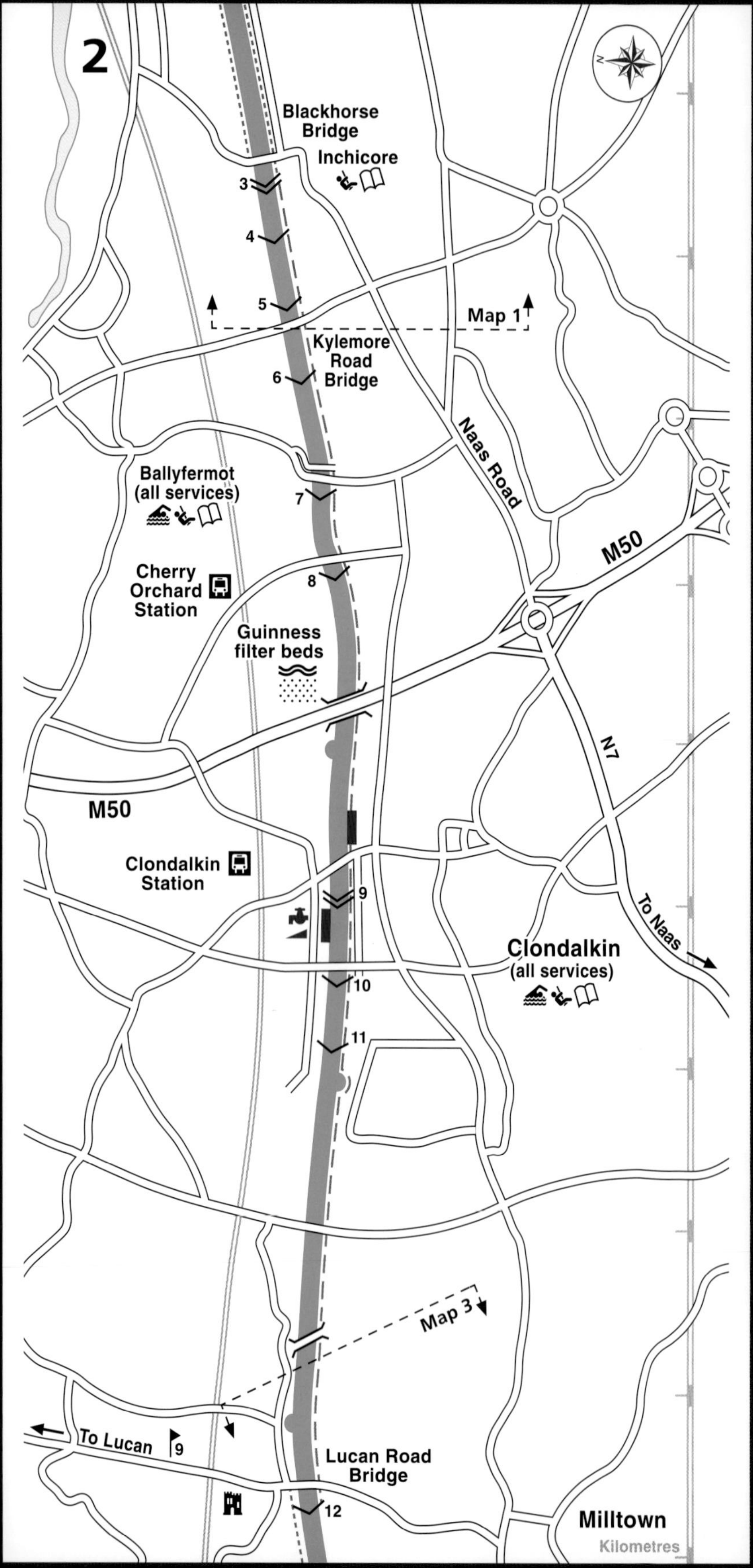

2

Blackhorse
Bridge

Inchicore

3

4

5

Map 1

Kylemore
Road
Bridge

6

Naas Road

M50

Ballyfermot
(all services)

7

Cherry
Orchard
Station

8

Guinness
filter beds

N7

M50

Clondalkin
Station

9

Clondalkin
(all services)

To Naas

10

11

Map 3

To Lucan 9

Lucan Road
Bridge

12

Milltown

Kilometres

SECTION 2 Blackhorse Bridge, Inchicore to 12th Lock, Lucan Road Bridge

Route Description

The canal rises steeply out of the city, parallel to the shared pedestrian / cycle path known as the Green Route and some points along the route are subject to anti-social behaviour. It is best to navigate the route from early in the morning to minimise the likelihood of unwanted attention, although this

has been mitigated by the installation of monitored CCTV along the entire Green Route. As the canal traverses this built up area, extra care is required as rubbish / debris may be present below the water surface. Some rubbish may be picked up by propellers, especially on deep-draught vessels through this stretch.

Above 8th Lock at the Park West Business Park, one can see water-retention ponds. These were used by Messrs Guinness when they used to take water out of the Grand Canal and hold it in these tanks prior to passing it through adjoining filter beds to achieve the level of purity that was required for brewing the perfect pint. The filter beds were filled in by Dublin Corporation, but the retention ponds remain, and have become a magnet for wildlife in the area beside Park West Business Park.

Above 11th Lock the canal at last emerges into a more rural setting, although the Green Route continues to Lock 12.

Facilities

All Services: Clondalkin; Ballyfermot
Water, Slip: 9th Lock, Clondalkin

History

Just below 8th Lock, a passage boat filled and sank one Christmas evening in 1792 with the loss of 11 lives. The accident was said to have been caused by the riotous behaviour of the passengers.

Clondalkin has a fine round tower, a large stone cross and the remains of an early monastery.

11th Lock was the first lock to be built by Thomas Omer in 1756. He started here because it was more difficult and expensive to buy land near the city. Omer envisaged a canal on a larger scale, and his three locks (11 to 13) were subsequently shortened by half and the width reduced by narrowing each end. The remains of the original tailgate recesses are still visible below 11th and 12th Locks. A small two-storied house above 11th Lock is typical of Omer's lock-houses. Lucan Road Bridge crosses the lower half of Omer's Lock and a short distance above 12th Lock there is another of his lock-houses. There were formerly many mills between here and the city but Grange Mills is the only one to have survived. Adamstown Castle, a 16th Century tower house, lies to the north of 12th Lock between the canal and the railway.

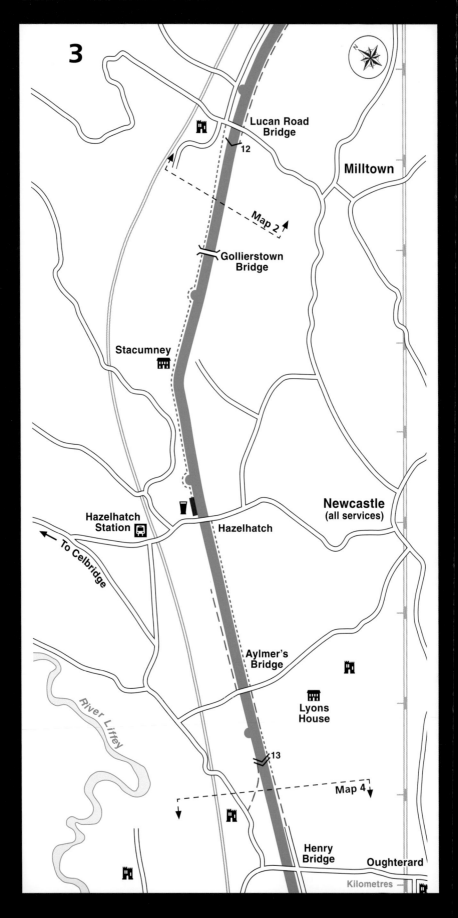

3

Lucan Road
Bridge

12

Milltown

Map 2

Gollierstown
Bridge

Stacumney

Hazelhatch
Station

To Celbridge

Hazelhatch

Newcastle
(all services)

Aylmer's
Bridge

Lyons
House

River Liffey

13

Map 4

Henry
Bridge

Oughterard

Kilometres

SECTION 3   12th Lock Lucan Road Bridge to Henry Bridge, Ardclough

Route Description

From 12th Lock the canal gradually enters a cutting as it approaches Gollierstown Bridge. Having emerged from the cutting at Stacumney, the canal is carried on an embankment towards Hazelhatch Bridge. There are fine views from the embankment of the Dublin mountains away to the south. Caution is required where there is a solid obstruction approximately 15 metres west of Hazelhatch Bridge, north of the channel centre.

Passing under Aylmer's Bridge, the canal skirts Lyons Demesne with its many fine trees. Part of the estate is an agricultural college for University College Dublin.

Celbridge Paddlers Canoe Club is situated at Aylmer's Bridge.

Facilities

All Services: Newcastle, 2 miles (3km) south from Hazelhatch Bridge
Pub: Hazelhatch

History

Omer deliberately routed his canal through the limestone quarries at Gollierstown, as this made it easier to transport the stone which was to be used for building locks and bridges along the line. By doing so, however, he added greatly to the difficulties of constructing the canal itself. John Smeaton, the eminent civil engineer, who visited Ireland in 1773 at the request of the newly-formed Grand Canal Company, criticised him for this decision.

Omer, like many other early canal engineers, did not follow contours, hence the cuttings and embankments which are features of this stretch of canal.

There was a store-yard and another of Omer's lock-houses at Stacumney. Known locally as "the hulk", it was at one time leased to people visiting nearby Lucan Spa to partake of the waters. Hazelhatch Bridge was originally made of wood but it was replaced by this handsome stone bridge when it was reported that passengers were in danger if they did not duck smartly. Newcastle was a garrison town for the Norman "Pale" and has an interesting early church tower, old glebe house and castle. The "Pale" was a boundary consisting essentially of a fortified ditch and rampart built around parts of medieval Meath, Dublin, Louth and Kildare to encompass the lands in control of the English settlers and removed from the land outside occupied by the native Irish.

Lyons House was formerly the home of the Cloncurrys. The 2nd Lord Cloncurry, who died in 1853, played an active part in the political and economic growth of the country and was one of the early directors of the canal company. There are a number of interesting castles in the area, constructed to protect the "Pale", one being in the Lyons Estate.

Valentine Lawless, the 2nd Lord Cloncurry was responsible for creating the Lyons Estate in the late 1790s. Part of the estate is now agricultural college for University College Dublin and part is being developed as a leisure centre.

In order to correct an error in the levels, an extra lock had to be built between Hazelhatch and Aylmer's Bridge. In 1783 this extra lock was removed and 13th Lock, the next one down the line, was converted into a double lock. The large lower gate recesses and the strange shape of the upper chamber are remnants of Omer's original larger lock. There was once a large mill above the lock, but this was destroyed by fire. Aylmer's and Henry Bridges record the names of local landlords who possibly financed the building or assisted the company in the purchase of land for the canal.

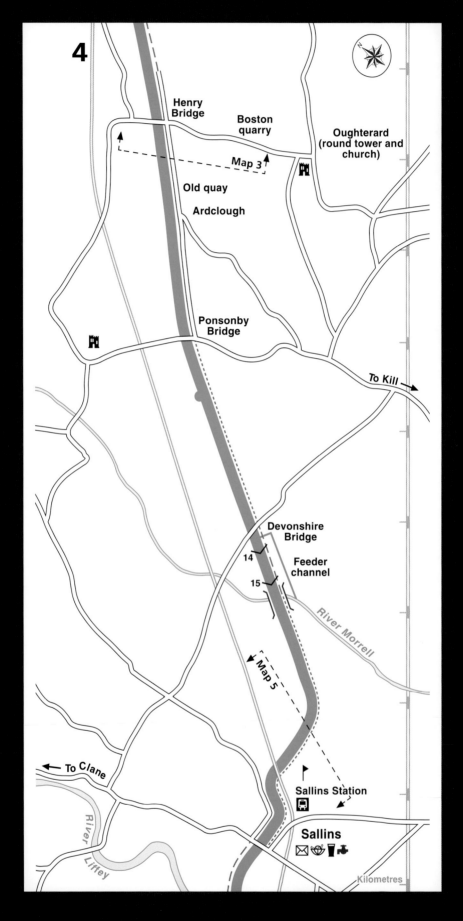

SECTION 4   Henry Bridge to Sallins

Route Description

Ponsonby Bridge was known to old canal men as "the eleven mile bridge" - probably 11 Irish miles from James's Street Harbour. The next stretch of canal is again embanked.

The Morrell Feeder enters from the south beyond Devonshire Bridge and care should be taken to allow for the current. The feeder is a short artificial cut which is taken from the River Morrell, a tributary of the Liffey and controlled by a sluice near the old lock-house beside 15th Lock.

Above 15th Lock the canal crosses the Morrell by a small aqueduct. A secluded and well-wooded stretch of canal follows and, passing under the main railway line from Dublin to Cork, the canal enters Sallins. The narrow road bridge over the canal was sensitively widened by Kildare County Council in 1988.

Facilities

Shops, Pubs, Post Office, Water: Sallins

History

At Oughterard there is an interesting ruined church and round tower. Arthur Guinness, founder of Guinness's Brewery in 1759, who "departed this life on 23rd January 1803" is buried here. Ardclough was once a busy hamlet serving the nearby Boston Quarry but the overgrown quay is now scarcely discernible.

It was the anticipation of obtaining water from the Morrell for the thirsty citizens of Dublin which prompted Dublin Corporation to take an active part in the construction of the canal in the early years. The supply began in 1777 and continued to be the principal source of drinking water until the Vartry scheme came into operation in 1869.

The canal company fought the construction of railways and raised all sorts of objections about the railway bridge but the railways expanded and all passenger traffic ceased on the canal in 1852.

Near Sallins, on the north bank, is what is reputed to be the first mass concrete building erected in Ireland, built by a French company as a sugar processing plant. Close to the bridge at Sallins was an old canal hotel, now demolished. Built in the 1780s by the canal company, it was too near Dublin and was never a commercial success. It was at the bridge at Sallins on 21 January 1777 that the directors of the canal company arrived in 10 post-chaises to receive the resignation of John Trail, their engineer, who had failed to carry out his contract to complete the canal to the Liffey.

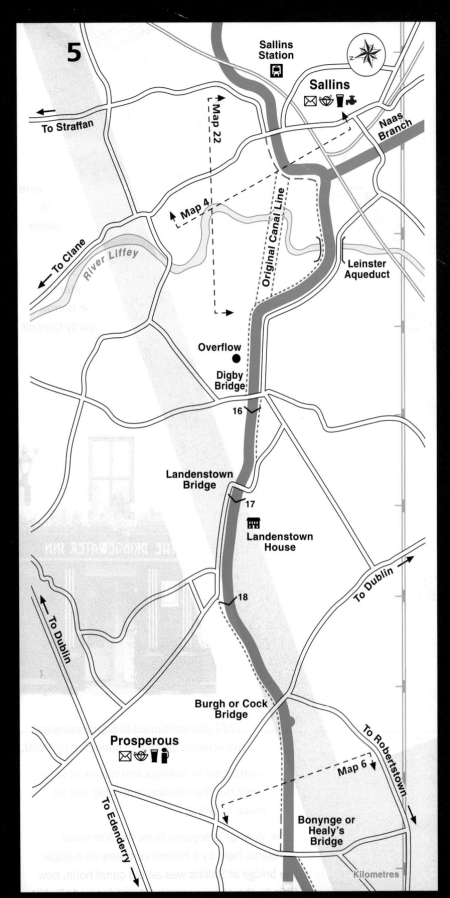

5

Sallins
Station

Sallins

Naas
Branch

To Straffan

Map 22

Map 4

To Clane

River Liffey

Original Canal Line

Leinster
Aqueduct

Overflow

Digby
Bridge

16

Landenstown
Bridge

17

Landenstown
House

18

To Dublin

To Dublin

Burgh or Cock
Bridge

Prosperous

To Robertstown

Map 6

To Edenderry

Bonynge or
Healy's
Bridge

Kilometres

SECTION 5   Sallins to Bonynge or Healy's Bridge

Route Description

Not far from Sallins the canal makes a double bend in preparation for the Liffey crossing, passing an old dry dock and Soldier's Island, the entrance to the Naas Branch (Sections 22 and 23). The Leinster Aqueduct is a fine structure and a short walk upstream reveals a good view of it. A footpath under the aqueduct links the towpaths on the north and south banks of the canal. The Liffey rises only 24km from Dublin but curves around taking 147km to reach the sea, and at this point it is flowing north.

Between the aqueduct and Digby Bridge there is an overflow on the north bank. Built in four circular basins to prevent erosion, it was known to the canal men as "the big pot, the little pot, the boolawn and the skillet".

At 17th Lock are the entrance gates to Landenstown House and the canal skirts the demesne lined by magnificent beeches. This is the headquarters of the Prosperous Angling Club and there is good coarse fishing. The village lies 3km to the north.

18th Lock is the last rising lock and a summit level of 9km lies ahead. The towpath between 18th Lock and Cock Bridge can be very wet and muddy in winter. The canal gradually narrows as it nears Cock Bridge and enters a cutting with overhanging trees. The canal has been passing around the Hill of Downings which contains a particularly good type of clay for lining the canal. Beyond Cock Bridge there are signs of extensive clay workings.

Facilities

Shops, Garage, Pubs, Post Office: Prosperous, about 3km north of 18th Lock

History

Omer originally intended to cross the Liffey downstream and a walk from the first bend after Sallins towards the river will reveal signs of his excavations and preparations for a lock.

The Naas Branch was completed to the town of Naas in 1789 by another company but it ran into financial difficulties and was taken over by the Grand Canal Company.

The Leinster Aqueduct was built by Richard Evans who later joined the Royal Canal Company and was the engineer of much of its early works.

Shortly after the canal was opened, side chambers were built at 16th and 17th Locks to conserve water as the supply from the Morrell proved to be insufficient. Much later the Grand Canal Company built a pumping station at the Leinster Aqueduct to raise water from the Liffey to the canal. This was taken over shortly afterwards (1947) by the Electricity Supply Board when it agreed to accept the responsibility for maintaining a navigable depth of water in return for extracting water from the canal for the cooling tower of the power station at Allenwood. The pumps were taken over by Waterways Ireland's predecessors after the closure of the power station and were refurbished to modern standards in 2012.

Landenstown House was built for the Digby family about 1740; Simon Digby MP was one of the early directors of the company.

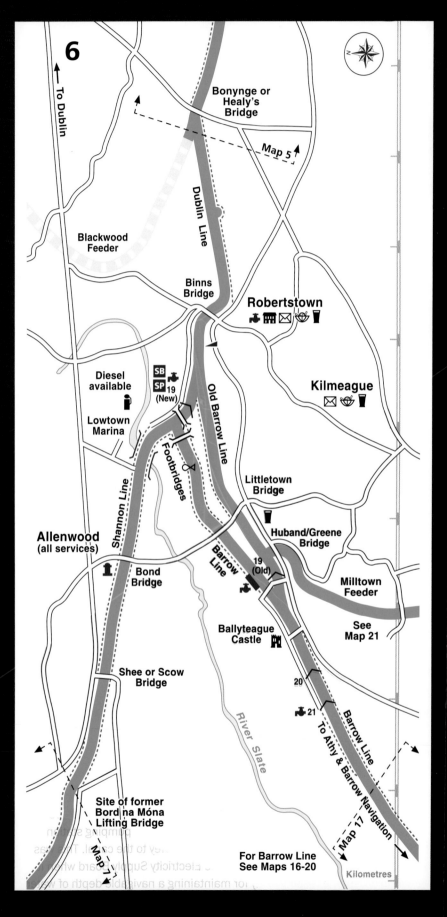

6

To Dublin

Bonynge or
Healy's
Bridge

Map 5

Dublin Line

Blackwood
Feeder

Binns
Bridge

Robertstown

Diesel
available

SB
SP 19
(New)

Old Barrow Line

Kilmeague

Lowtown
Marina

Footbridges

Littletown
Bridge

Shannon Line

Huband/Greene
Bridge

Allenwood
(all services)

Barrow
Line

19
(Old)

Milltown
Feeder

Bond
Bridge

See
Map 21

Ballyteague
Castle

Shee or Scow
Bridge

20

River Slate

21

Barrow Line

To Athy & Barrow Navigation

Map 17

Site of former
Bord na Móna
Lifting Bridge

For Barrow Line
See Maps 16-20

Kilometres

SECTION 6   Bonynge or Healy's Bridge to Site of former Bord na Móna Railway Bridge

Route Description

At Healy's Bridge the Blackwood water supply used to enter the canal; 6.5km long, it was a controlled supply, fed by an artificial reservoir. The Blackwood Feeder was closed in 1952 and sold off. It is now partly filled in. The reservoir, Ballinafagh Lake, is one of the largest bodies of water in Co Kildare and owing to its high ecological value, has been designated a candidate SAC.

The canal is carried on an embankment through the Bog of Moods to Robertstown.

Below the new 19th Lock, the canal stores have been converted into a boatyard facility called Lowtown Marina. The new Barrow Line branches off to the south and the Main Line continues on over two small aqueducts, the first of these over the Slate which is good for trout fishing.

The local community in Allenwood has developed an interesting series of linked walking routes using the canal towpath, forest tracks and paths across the bogs.

Above the old 19th Lock, the end of the summit level, the old Barrow Line carrying water from the Milltown supply joins the Main Line. The feeder is navigable to Milltown Bridge (about 10km) for very shallow draught boats but is obstructed by a low bridge (about 1.95m) near Kilmeague. It continues on to springs near Pollardstown, whose crystal clear waters are the canal's principal supply (Section 21).

Facilities
All Services: Allenwood
Shops, Pubs, Post Office: Robertstown and Kilmeague
Water, Slip: Robertstown, west of Binn's Bridge
Water, Fuel, Pump-out Station, Service Block: Lock 19, Main Line
Water: New Barrow Line (west of Old Lock 19) and Lock 21
Pub: Littletown Bridge

History
The early engineers did not allow for subsidence in crossing the Bog of Moods, a mistake they repeated at the bog west of Ticknevin. Subsidence of up to 4.9m occurred and in the end the canal had to be carried on a high embankment.

Robertstown Hotel was opened in 1801 and an extension was added in 1804. Business was good in the early days, but revenue began to fall in 1808. Gradually the 72 windows and 62 hearths were closed up to avoid paying tax. In 1849 it ceased to be a hotel. In 1869, after long negotiations, the building was leased to the Royal Irish Constabulary, who used it as a barracks until 1905. In more recent years it has had a number of uses and it is now in private ownership.

A coalyard was constructed in 1808 at Lowtown by the Grand Canal Company, from which coal could be carried east into Dublin or west to Tullamore. This was in conjunction with the leasing of the collieries near Castlecomer in an attempt to increase trade.

Shee Bridge, known locally as "Scow Bridge" (probably a corruption of "skew") is the only oblique-arched bridge on the canal, apart from the later railway arch at Ringsend.

Passing close to Allenwood village, the canal nears the site of an old ESB power station, which, when in use, drew water from the canal. The giant cooling tower has been demolished. The location of the Bord na Móna guillotine bridge, constructed to convey turf by light rail to the power station, is still clearly visible.

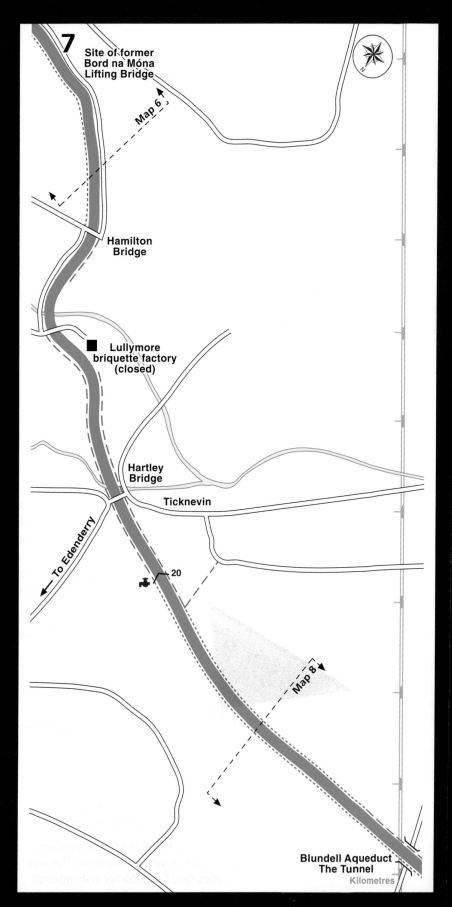

7

Site of former
Bord na Móna
Lifting Bridge

Map 6

Hamilton
Bridge

Lullymore
briquette factory
(closed)

Hartley
Bridge

Ticknevin

To Edenderry

20

Map 8

Blundell Aqueduct
The Tunnel

Kilometres

SECTION 7 — Site of former Bord na Móna Railway Bridge to Blundell Aqueduct

Route Description

The stretch to Hamilton Bridge is very popular with local and visiting fishermen. It is interesting to compare the style of the 1796 Hamilton Bridge with the 1949 Kilpatrick Bridge.

This is a pretty section especially when the hawthorn is in bloom. Lock 20 ends this 11km level and the canal stretches away into the distance across the bog without another lock for 30km. The canal skirts the northern limit of the bog with poor scrub to the north. Blundell Aqueduct, known locally as the Tunnel, carries the canal across the Edenderry-Rathangan road.

Facilities

Water: Lock 20

History

There have been many efforts over the years to exploit the bogs. In the 1850s the Irish Amelioration Society set up works near Allenwood to make charcoal out of turf, without much success. The briquette factory was erected in 1934 but ran into financial and technical trouble and was taken over by the Turf Development Board, the forerunner of Bord na Móna. It was closed in 1993.

20th Lock used to have side-chambers and the hole in the wall of the chamber is visible but the ponds have been filled in.

One tends to think of aqueducts and tunnels as the most impressive and difficult canal works but this stretch of canal across the bog was one of the most difficult engineering feats ever attempted before or, indeed, since. It took nearly ten years to complete and many times the engineers felt like abandoning it for another route. These engineers, including John Smeaton, did not anticipate the enormous subsidence. Smeaton advised that the canal should be run through the bog at the original level, time was not allowed for subsidence and, once again, the engineers were faced with the task of securing high embankments. Looking to the south one can see the land rising to the original level of the bog beyond the range of the drainage caused by the canal works. In order to construct the canal, a series of drains were opened, crossed by transverse drains, and the material excavated was dried in the squares created by the drains and was then wheeled to the canal to form the embankments. The channel along the top of the embankment was then lined with clay to hold the water in. The traveller today could well spare a thought for the men who laboured through ten winters to achieve this remarkable stretch of canal.

In recent years extensive reconstruction has been carried out to the bog embankments between 20th Lock and the Blundell Aqueduct. There is little trace to be seen above the water of these major engineering works which will maintain the stability of the embankments for future years.

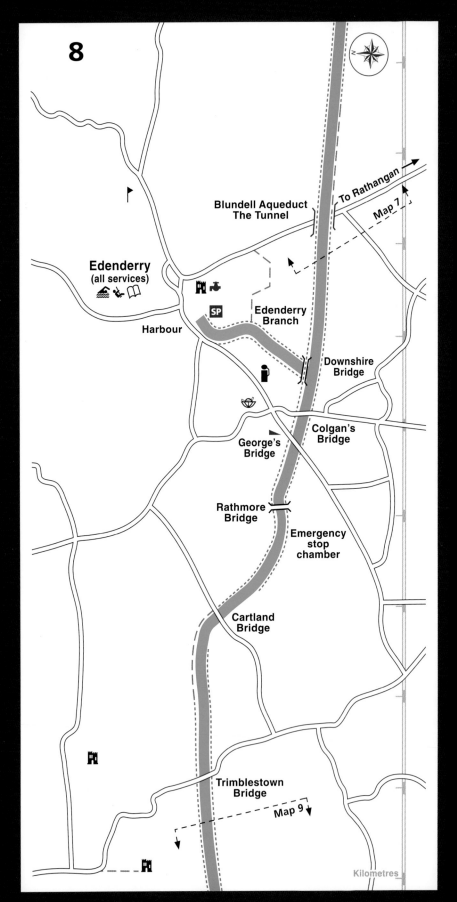

8

Blundell Aqueduct
The Tunnel

To Rathangan

Map 7

Edenderry
(all services)

SP

Edenderry
Branch

Harbour

Downshire
Bridge

Colgan's
Bridge

George's
Bridge

Rathmore
Bridge

Emergency
stop
chamber

Cartland
Bridge

Trimblestown
Bridge

Map 9

Kilometres

SECTION 8 Blundell Aqueduct to Trimblestown Bridge

Route Description

Due to the shallow sloping sides of the canal between the Blundell Aqueduct and Downshire Bridge, boats should keep to the centre of the channel and away from the banks.

The canal continues, carried on a high embankment, to the entrance to the Edenderry Branch. This canal is 1.5km long without any locks and winds its way up to an attractive harbour in the heart of the town. Approaching Colgan's Bridge, the crossing of the bog accomplished, the scenery returns to the familiar hedgerows.

Colgan's Bridge and George's Bridge are close together. The latter has been replaced by a modern structure which presents an ugly appearance to the canal and one feels that the engineers reluctantly allowed sufficient headroom for the boats.

For the next few miles the canal seems to detach itself from the busy world. Rathmore Bridge serves no road - it is an accommodation bridge, built to accommodate the farmer whose land was divided when the canal was cut. An emergency stop chamber was constructed immediately west of Rathmore Bridge and should a breach occur in the future, the stop-gates are designed to close, limiting the loss of water from the canal and the damage to the embankments. Ballybrittan Castle is about 1.5km to the north of Trimblestown Bridge.

Facilities

All Services: Edenderry
Shop: at crossroads just north of Colgan's or George's Bridge
Slip: George's Bridge, Edenderry
Garage: on Edenderry Road
Water, Pump-Out Station: Edenderry

History

The embankment between the Blundell Aqueduct and the Edenderry Branch has caused a great deal of trouble over the years. A few hundred yards west of the aqueduct, on the north bank, major breaches occurred in 1797, shortly after the canal was opened, and in 1800, 1916 and 1989. The latest breach in 1989 was by far the most serious, and took about one year to repair at a cost of over IR£1 million. The embankment had to be rebuilt and the channel relined using modern materials to prevent seepage. In an innovative measure, aquatic reeds were transplanted along the water's edge of the repaired section. The plants help to prevent bank erosion by absorbing the wave energy caused by boats and wind and they create an important habitat for fish, birds and aquatic invertebrates.

The Edenderry Branch, financed by the local landlord, Lord Downshire, was built at the same time as the Main Line but the harbour was not finally completed until 1802. On a hill near the harbour stands the ruins of Blundell Castle. Lord Downshire married into the Blundell family and he proved a good landlord carrying out many improvements in the town.

At Drumcooley, on the south bank, opposite the entrance to the Edenderry Branch, there was a peat litter factory until 1945. It was started by Norman Palmer who originally conveyed turf to a factory in an old mill at 2nd Lock in Dublin but, when it was burnt down, he moved operations to Drumcooley.

Colgan was the name of the owner of the house at the bridge who kept a waiting room for passengers in the old days. On one occasion he was reprimanded for failing to keep it open when a young lady passenger found herself deposited "at 11 o'clock of a dark night without any certainty of protection".

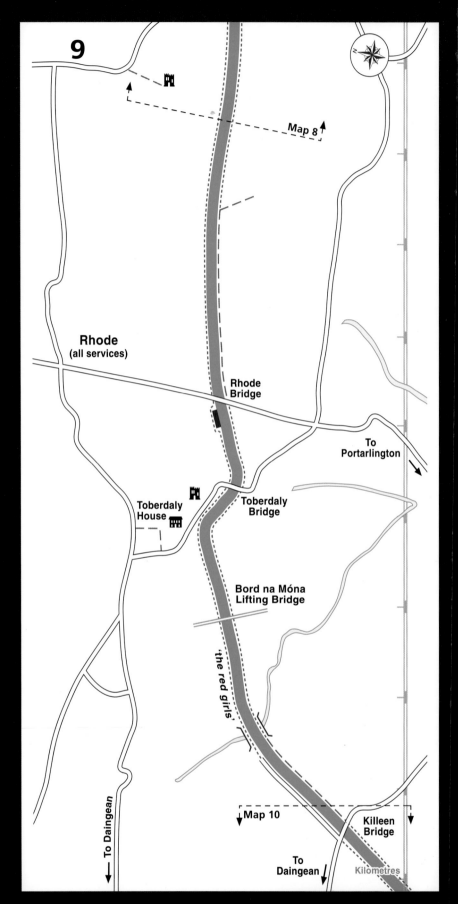

9

Map 8

Rhode
(all services)

Rhode
Bridge

To
Portarlington

Toberdaly
House

Toberdaly
Bridge

Bord na Móna
Lifting Bridge

'the red girls'

To Daingean

Map 10

Killeen
Bridge

To
Daingean

Kilometres

SECTION 9   Trimblestown Bridge to Killeen Bridge

Route Description

This is a very attractive stretch of canal with some forestry planting on the south side. There is a quay west of Rhode Bridge and from here it is about 1.5km to the village of Rhode. Approaching Toberdaly Bridge there are some attractive stone cottages on the south side which must have been part of Toberdaly estate and the ruins of the castle may be seen on the hill to the north. Croghan Hill has a prehistoric cairn on the summit is a prominent feature. The canal takes a surprisingly sharp bend into Toberdaly Bridge.

Soon the trees give way to scrub land and more bog lies ahead with another light railway bridge. This bridge is in frequent use and has to be raised for boats to pass. There are mooring facilities both sides of the bridge on the north bank. The bridge is left open for boats when not in use.

Facilities

All Services: Rhode, 1.5km north of Rhode Bridge

History

Toberdaly Castle is well worth a visit, there are some people living in the houses in the yard who will allow you to look around. Apart from the castle, there seems to be ruins of other buildings dating from different periods with walled enclosures sloping down to the canal.

Photo courtesy: Conor Nolan

Near Killeen Bridge there is a stretch known to the old canal men as "The Red Girls" because at one time a family of auburn-haired beauties lived in a house along the bank.

Turf used to be one of the principal commodities carried on the canal and, during the "emergency years" in the 1940s, over 200,000 tons were shipped to Dublin in specially built boats. Recent development of the bogs has made no use of the canal but has used a network of light railways. The modern system, which is also used in Russia, is to pulverise the turf, air dry it and then transport it to the nearby power station where it is blown into the furnaces at pressure.

One severe, cold and wet night in 1836, a turf boat went aground near Killeen Bridge because the long level was lowered by an exceptionally strong west wind. The crew refused to lighten the load to move her and a passage boat was held up for six hours until a boat arrived from the opposite direction and they were able to transfer the passengers.

The Rhode Power plant was shut down in 2003 and its cooling towers were demolished in March 2004, removing a highly visible landmark.

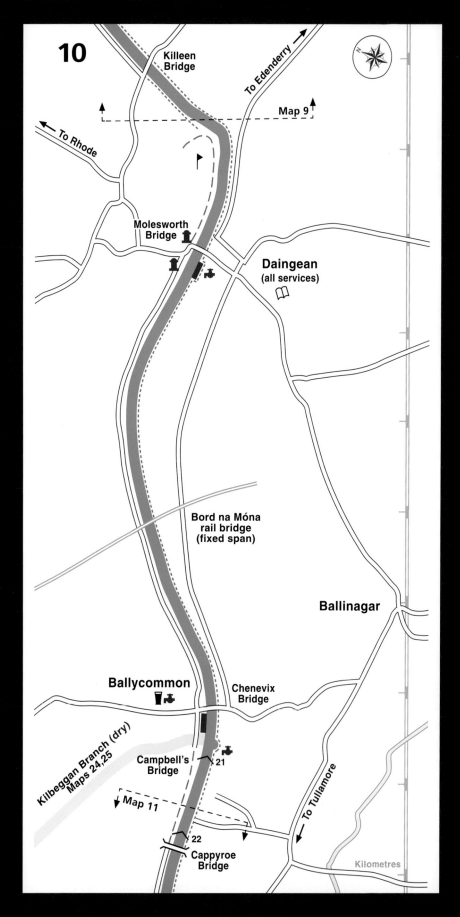

10

Killeen
Bridge

To Edenderry →

Map 9

← To Rhode

Molesworth
Bridge

Daingean
(all services)

Bord na Móna
rail bridge
(fixed span)

Ballinagar

Ballycommon

Chenevix
Bridge

Kilbeggan Branch (dry)
Maps 24,25

Campbell's
Bridge

21

To Tullamore

↓ Map 11

22

Cappyroe
Bridge

Kilometres

SECTION 10

Killeen Bridge to Ballycommon

Route Description

The canal converges with the main Edenderry-Tullamore road about 1.5km from Daingean. There is a quay west of Molesworth Bridge in Daingean. On the opposite side of the canal are the forbidding walls of a former reformatory, now used as a store by the National Museum. The town is small, with a number of mooring options - advice on mooring should be sought from the local Lockkeeper.

Leaving Daingean the canal passes through scrub land, poor agriculturally but rich in wildlife. There is a Bord na Móna fixed-span crossing for the light-rail system here. The canal enters a short cutting and then the land falls away to the south as it approaches Ballycommon. There is a convenient quay to the west of Chenevix Bridge.

A short distance below the bridge the Kilbeggan Branch (13km long with no locks) used to join the Main Line but the entrance was sealed off and the bed is dry (Sections 24 and 25). The fine Kilbeggan Harbour buildings have been restored by the Kilbeggan Harbour Amenity Group who, along with the Ballycommon Canal Renewal Group, Offaly IWAI and the Heritage Boat Association, have been campaigning to have this fine stretch of waterway rewatered and reopened.

Facilities

All Services: Daingean
Water, Pub: Ballycommon
Water: Lock 21 and Molesworth Bridge

History

Daingean used to be the stronghold of the local chieftains, the O'Connors. In the 16th Century, during the reign of Philip and Mary, the town was renamed Philipstown. It was once the assize town for the county but this position was usurped in 1833 by the rapidly expanding town of Tullamore and thereafter Philipstown declined in importance. In 1920 the town reverted to its original name. The court house is attributed to the architect James Gandon.

Photo courtesy: Giles Byford

There used to be a sunken hull of an old flyboat here but it was removed some years ago. If, as the local people say, the flyboat was the Hibernia, she was built in 1832 at Ringsend Iron Works by Courtney Clark. She was an imitation of the successful boats designed for the Paisley Canal by Houston but, although constructed of one-eighth-inch sheet iron, she proved too heavy to reach the critical speed of 12km/h required to make her rise on her own bow wave and eventually the canal company was forced to order hulls from Scotland.

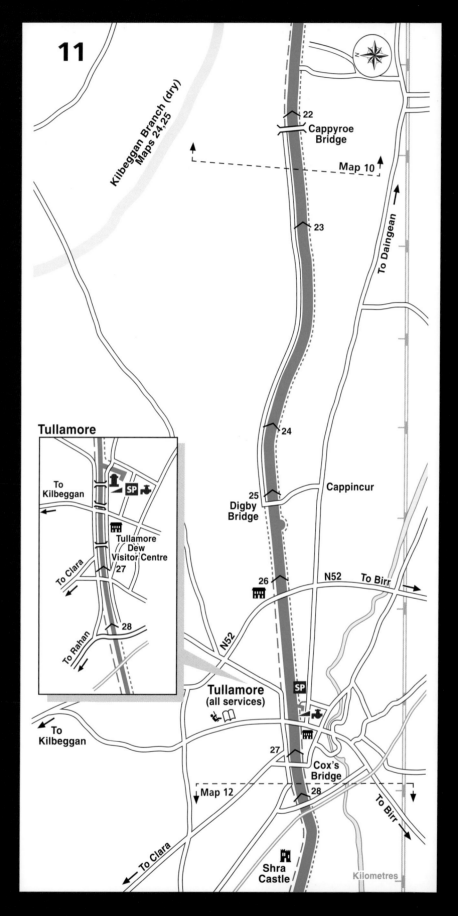

11

Kilbeggan Branch (dry)
Maps 24,25

22
Cappyroe Bridge

Map 10

23

To Daingean

24

Cappincur

25
Digby Bridge

N52   To Birr

26

Tullamore

To Kilbeggan

SP

Tullamore Dew Visitor Centre

27

To Clara

28

To Rahan

N52

Tullamore
(all services)

SP

27

Cox's Bridge

Map 12   28

To Birr

To Kilbeggan

To Clara

Shra Castle

Kilometres

SECTION 11   Ballycommon to Tullamore

Route Description

After travelling so many miles on the long level, the drop down into Tullamore seems to be very steep. Offaly Rowing Club is based just below the 23rd Lock and regularly trains on the stretch between its base and Lock 24.

The memory of Mike and Heather Thomas, owners of Celtic Canal Cruisers, is honoured at 25th Lock with an inscribed granite seat erected by the IWAI Offaly Branch.

The towpath between Cappincur and Tullamore is a pleasant walk, much frequented by the residents of the town. The stretch between Bolands Lock and the beautiful restored Round House at Lock 26, and the town, provides a linear tree lined entrance to Tullamore.

The best moorings in Tullamore are up the short branch to the north of the enclosed harbour. This is now the central engineering depot for the canal but suitable mooring has been provided for visiting boats outside the harbour. The shopping centre of the town lies to the south of the canal. The quay on the Main Line was formerly used by D.E. Williams, makers of the legendary Tullamore Dew and Irish Mist Whiskey.

Facilities

All Services: Tullamore
Slip, Pumpout, Water: Tullamore

History

26th Lock is known locally as "Bolands Lock" after the Boland family who lived there at one time. The lock-house is known as "the Round House". It was built by the contractor, Michael Hayes, on his own initiative and the directors refused to meet the "extraordinary and unnecessary" extra expense of £427.11 d. Timber supports were put into the lock in 1812 because it was "bulging dangerously" and it was decided to postpone the permanent repair until a "more convenient season"! The lock was repaired in 1993, and the timber supports finally removed. In 1999 the lock-house was restored and is now open to the public at selected times.

Tullamore was the terminus of the canal for a number of years while the directors argued about how the line should be continued to the Shannon and this is why they decided to build a harbour here. It originally contained a magnificent range of warehouses but these were demolished in the 1940s. The attractive canal hotel on the branch was built in 1800-1801 by the same contractor, Michael Hayes. It ceased to operate as a hotel in the 1830s and it was used as a presbytery from 1859 until 1974. Sadly it was then demolished to make way for a modern presbytery.

The Tullamore Dew Visitors Centre is located in the 1897 bonded warehouse on the canal bank at Bury Quay. Visitors can wander through the various recreated working stations that were at the Tullamore Dew distillery such as malting, bottling or cooperage areas and learn how the whiskey was made, followed by complimentary tasting of Tullamore Dew Whiskey. The Tourist Office is also in this building.

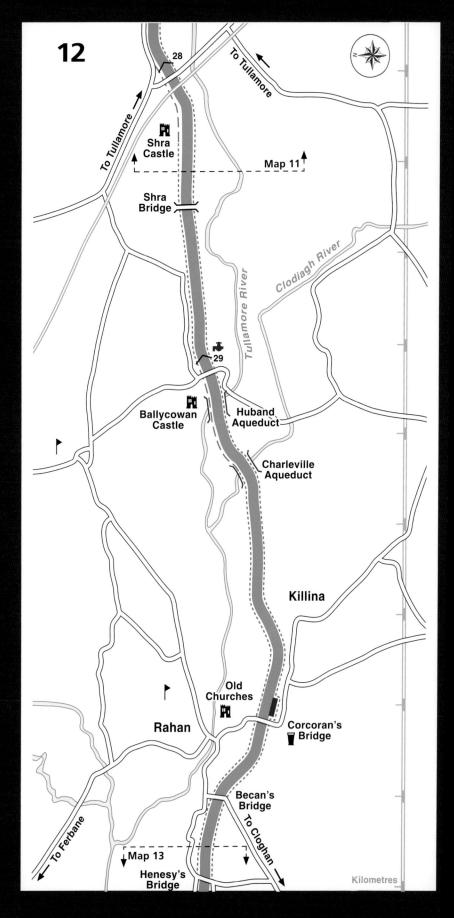

12

28

To Tullamore

To Tullamore

Shra
Castle

Map 11

Shra
Bridge

Tullamore River

Clodiagh River

29

Ballycowan
Castle

Huband
Aqueduct

Charleville
Aqueduct

Killina

Old
Churches

Corcoran's
Bridge

Rahan

Becan's
Bridge

To Ferbane

To Cloghan

Map 13

Henesy's
Bridge

Kilometres

SECTION 12 Tullamore to Henesy's Bridge, Rahan

Route Description

After passing under the Dublin-Athlone railway bridge, the canal curves around Shra Castle, passing an interesting old graveyard on the way to Ballycowan.

Just below 29th Lock, known locally as "Patsy's Lock", the canal crosses the Tullamore River by the Huband Aqueduct and the fine ruins of Ballycowan Castle are close by.

Rounding another bend, the canal crosses the Clodiagh River by the Charleville Aqueduct. A short distance west is the site of the old Rahan footbridge. The bridge became unsafe and the span over the canal was removed in 1992. All that remains now are the concrete abutments which mark the bridge position.

Further west is a convenient quay to moor while visiting Rahan churches. Rahan village lies a short distance to the north of the canal. The Thatch pub, dating back to the 1700's, is located on the eastern side of Corcoran's bridge.

Facilities

Pub: near Corcoran's Bridge
Water: Lock 29

History

Shra Castle was built by an Elizabethan officer, John Brisco, in 1588. Ballycowan Castle, built by Sir Jasper Herbert in 1626, is on the site of an earlier castle.

Huband Aqueduct is named after a prominent director, Joseph Huband, a barrister, who was elected in 1777 and, with the exception of a few years, remained a director until 1835. Charleville Aqueduct was named after Lord Charleville, a prominent landowner. His castle lies to the south of the canal, built in 1801 to the designs of Francis Johnston.

The Corcoran family were the owners of The Thatch and at one time Mr Corcoran acted as agent to the company. In 1838 he reported that 350 passengers had used his station.

Rahan churches are attributed to St Cartach. The largest, said to date from about 1100, is still used by the Church of Ireland. Its stone-roofed chancel was originally flanked by chambers; its arch and the unique circular east window are romanesque. The nave was rebuilt in the 18th Century and the small church nearby is 15th Century with a romanesque doorway. Other items of interest locally are the stained glass windows by Evie Hone at St Stanislaus College, up until recently a Jesuit institution.

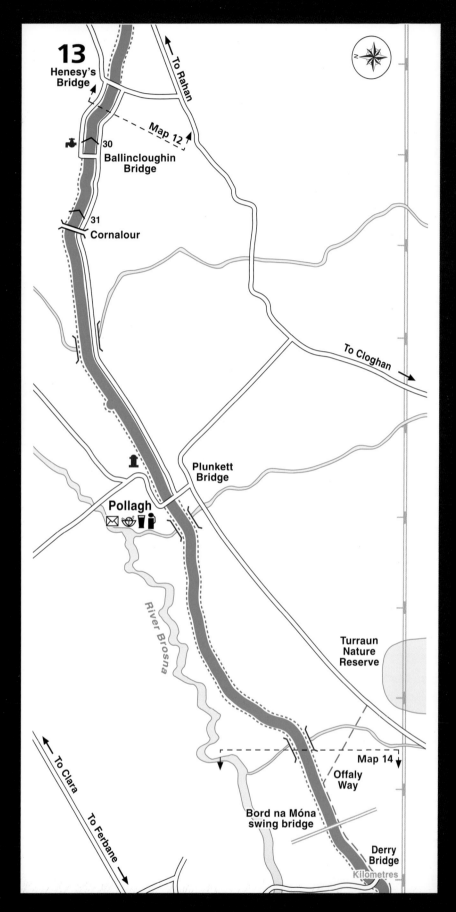

13

Henesy's
Bridge

To Rahan

Map 12

30
Ballincloughin
Bridge

31
Cornalour

To Cloghan

Plunkett
Bridge

Pollagh

River Brosna

Turraun
Nature
Reserve

To Ciara

To Ferbane

Map 14

Offaly
Way

Bord na Móna
swing bridge

Derry
Bridge

Kilometres

SECTION 13 Henesy's Bridge, Rahan to Derry Bridge

Route Description

Below 31st Lock at Cornalour the canal swings around a corner to set off on a long level of nearly 16km. When travelling east, towards Dublin, it is easy to round this corner after the long level and meet the bridge and lock unexpectedly.

On the north bank just east of Pollagh Bridge is the best place to moor. Pollagh has a quaint shaped church which contains carvings and furniture made of bog oak, as well as Harry Clarke stained glass windows, and is well worth visiting.

West of Pollagh occasional glimpses of the River Brosna may be seen to the north. Drainage operations some years ago have left ugly mounds which indicate the presence of the river. The land between the river and the canal is scrub - poor agricultural land but rich in wildlife. Away to the south the Slieve Bloom mountains break the monotony of the flat country. The Bord na Móna railway bridge is left open for boats.

Facilities

Shops, Garage, Pub, Post Office: Pollagh
Water: Lock 30

History

A glance at the map shows how closely the canal follows the River Brosna from Tullamore and it is interesting to note that Omer, the engineer who laid out the original line, planned to use the river. It was subsequently decided that a still-water navigation would be more practical.

The former Turraun peat works date back to the early 1900s and it was here that experiments were carried out in artificial methods of drying turf. It was eventually decided that air-drying was the most efficient and this is the method used today. The development of the bogs has brought about great changes in the area. A traveller along this stretch of canal in the 1830s described "the wretched hovels constructed of wet sods....the thatch is generally composed of rushes or stalks of the potato". Modern prosperity has long since swept such scenes away. The production of sod turf has ceased, and a nature reserve has been created from part of the cut-away bog at Turraun.

There is a local legend that St Manchan cast a penance on the people of Pollagh to provide free milk to travellers because somebody stole his cow and put it in the pot. This custom survived to the days of the canal men but today's traveller will have to pay.

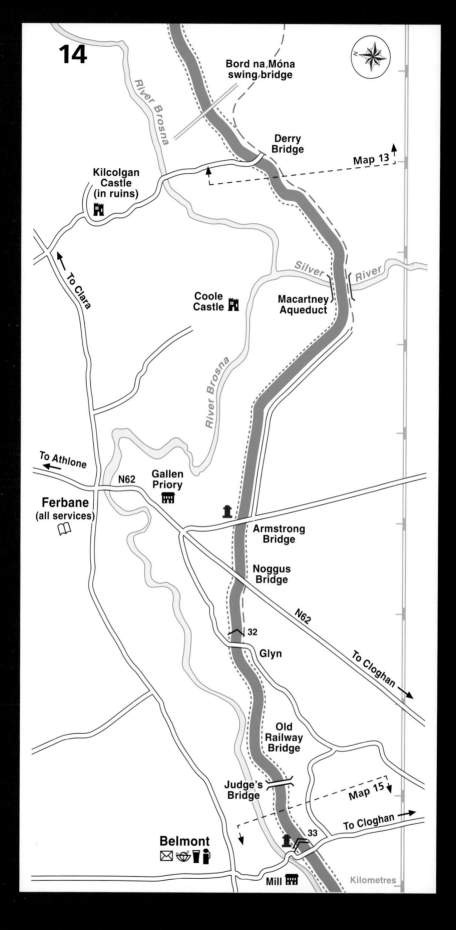

14

Bord na Móna
swing bridge

River Brosna

Derry
Bridge

Map 13

Kilcolgan
Castle
(in ruins)

To Clara

Silver River

Coole
Castle

Macartney
Aqueduct

River Brosna

To Athlone

N62

Gallen
Priory

Ferbane
(all services)

Armstrong
Bridge

Noggus
Bridge

N62

32

Glyn

To Cloghan

Old
Railway
Bridge

Judge's
Bridge

Map 15

To Cloghan

33

Belmont

Mill

Kilometres

SECTION 14   Derry Bridge to Belmont

Route Description

Because the canal curves around to cross the Silver River, there is an interesting view of Macartney Aqueduct in the distance.

There is an inspector's house and some old stables at Armstrong Bridge. From here the canal passes through a rock cutting to Noggus Bridge, another access point to Ferbane.

33rd Lock is a double and care is required where the bridge is built across the lower chamber. A short distance to the north there is a fine bridge across the Brosna and the 18th Century Belmont Mills, with the village of Belmont less than 1.5km from the canal.

Facilities

All Services: Ferbane, 3km north from Armstrong Bridge
Shops, Garage, Pubs, Post Office: Belmont, 1.5km north from 33rd Lock

History

Kilcolgan Castle, a Jacobean strong-house of the MacCoughlan family, lies about 2.5km to the north of Derry Bridge. The stones were taken for road materials and little remains but the bawn. Coole Castle is on the north bank of the Brosna almost due north from Macartney Aqueduct. It is a typical 15/16th Century tower house with interesting angle loops and triple spiral ventilators.

The engineers had learnt from the earlier mistakes in cutting the canal through bog. A much longer time was allowed for subsidence here and the canal was carried through at the new level of the bog. There have been problems here, however, and a major canal breach occurred near Derry Bridge in January 1954, taking four months to repair.

Macartney Aqueduct, named after Sir John Macartney, the chairman of the board who was knighted at the opening of Ringsend Docks, proved a difficult piece of engineering for the Grand Canal Company's John Killaly but it has stood the test of time well.

Gallen Priory is a gothicised Georgian house, formerly the home of the Armstrong family and now a convent. A monastery was founded here in the 5th Century by St Canoc, situated between the house and the river. In the middle ages it became an Augustinian priory and, although no traces of the buildings survive above ground, excavations have revealed a large number of grave slabs now mounted in the rebuilt gable wall of the excavated church. To the south across the river are the ruins of a 15th Century parish church which lay outside the monastery.

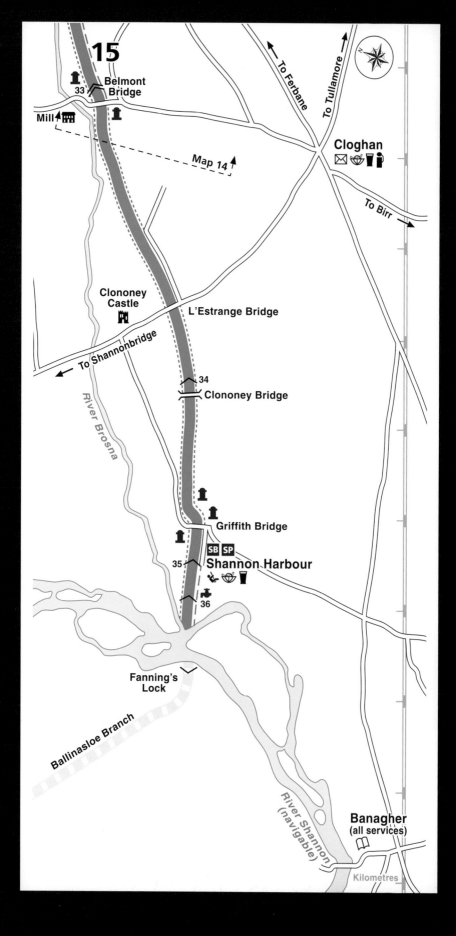

15

33

Belmont
Bridge

Mill

To Ferbane

To Tullamore

Cloghan

Map 14

To Birr

Clononey
Castle

L'Estrange Bridge

To Shannonbridge

River Brosna

34

Clononey Bridge

Griffith Bridge

SB SP

35

Shannon Harbour

36

Fanning's
Lock

Ballinasloe Branch

River Shannon
(navigable)

Banagher
(all services)

Kilometres

SECTION 15   Belmont to Shannon Harbour

Route Description

This level used to get rather shallow, because boats locking in and out of Shannon Harbour drew off the water. Now, during dry summers, water is back-pumped from the Shannon.

Griffith Bridge, bearing the rope marks of earlier years, is at the entrance to Shannon Harbour. Here one is very conscious of the past with the old hotel, buildings and warehouses. There is a waiting jetty below 36th Lock. The Brosna, entering the Shannon here, causes heavy silting and the deep channel is near the south bank. Travelling downstream on the Shannon, it is possible to mistake the entrance to the canal, which is to the south of the small island. Fanning's Lock, the entrance to the Ballinasloe Branch, is across the river. This branch line is now closed and much of it has disappeared in bog working.

Facilities

Shops, Garage, Pubs, Post Office: Cloghan
Shop, Pub, Service Block, Pump-out Station, Playground: Shannon Harbour
Water: Lock 35
All Services: Banagher

History

At L'Estrange Bridge are the ruins of a former inn. A short distance up the road to the north, there are large gates which led to a former military barracks, now demolished - one of a series built in the early 1800s to meet the threat of French invasion from the west. Less than 1km from the bridge along the same road is Clononey Castle. It has a well preserved bawn and a 16th Century tower house, which was restored in the last century by an eccentric lawyer. There is an interesting grave slab here, bearing the names of some of the Boleyn family, which is said to have been unearthed by workmen quarrying stone for the canal works.

The canal was completed in 1803 but considerable difficulty was experienced in staunching parts of it. A boat did pass through in April 1804 but it was not until 1805 that the link was permanently secured. The hotel at Shannon Harbour was completed in 1806 but was only successful for a short period when emigrants were making their way to the New World. The agent's house, a police barracks and some of the old warehouses remain. In 1946 the new loading shed was built and 35th and 36th Locks were enlarged. It is difficult to believe it now, but the harbour area was once bustling with activity, and large numbers of people were employed in various boat-related businesses.

The Ballinasloe Branch (23km long with two locks) was completed in 1828 and the remains of the old horse bridge across the Shannon are still visible. It was replaced by a ferry in 1849, which was abandoned when the boats were mechanised.

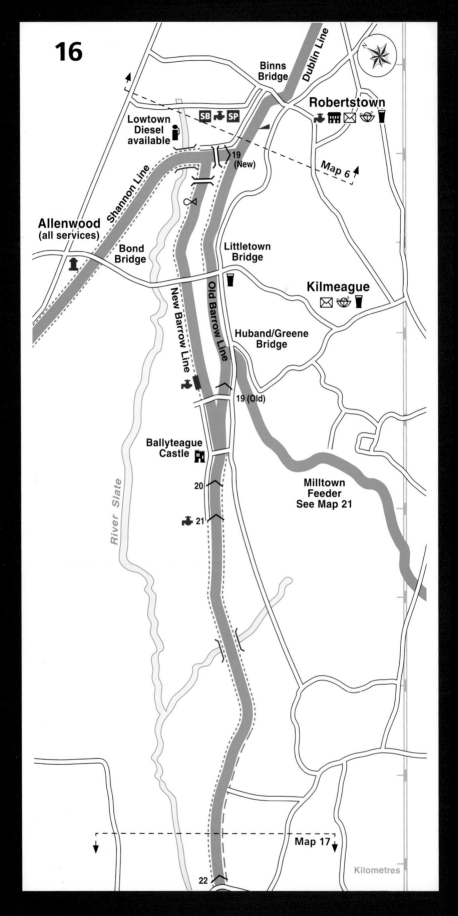

16

Binns
Bridge

Dublin Line

Robertstown

Lowtown
Diesel
available

SB SP

19
(New)

Map 6

Allenwood
(all services)

Shannon Line

Bond
Bridge

Littletown
Bridge

Kilmeague

New Barrow Line

Old Barrow Line

Huband/Greene
Bridge

19 (Old)

Ballyteague
Castle

20

Milltown
Feeder
See Map 21

21

River Slate

Map 17

Kilometres

22

MAPS & GUIDES 16 TO 20
BARROW LINE, LOWTOWN TO ATHY

SECTION 16   Lowtown to Glenaree Bridge

Route Description

The Barrow Line of the Grand Canal joins the Main Line a short distance below the old 19th Lock. The Milltown Feeder is navigable by shallow draft boats only, requiring limited headroom. Details of the Milltown Feeder are shown in Section 21. Passing down through 20th and 21st Locks, the canal crosses Ballyteague Bog and it is very exposed here in windy weather. Just north of the jetty at Ballyteague, on the new Barrow Line, there is a line of angling stands. Some of these were designed specifically for use by people with disabilities, and allow easy and safe access for wheelchair users to fish the canal.

Facilities

All Services: Allenwood
Shops, Pubs, Post Office: Robertstown and Kilmeague
Water, Slip: Robertstown, west of Binn's Bridge
Water, Fuel, Pump-out Station, Service Block: Lock 19, Main Line
Water: New Barrow Line (west of Old Lock 19) and Lock 21
Pub: Littletown Bridge

History

The bridge over the Milltown Feeder near the old 19th Lock presents a puzzle. On one side it bears the inscription Huband Bridge 1788 and on the other face, Greene Bridge 1799. Joseph Huband was one of the canal directors and Greene was an early secretary of the company.

The old Barrow Line, into which the Milltown Feeder flows, was the original line of the canal. The canal through Ballyteague Bog proved very difficult to construct and severe bog subsidence eventually forced the canal company to construct a new stretch of canal. In 1804 the new Barrow line was constructed. This became the only route for a time with the closure of the old 19th Lock in the 1860s. The old line was re-opened in 1973 to provide a circular route for local boats. Unfortunately the problems solved by the building of the new Barrow Line reappeared when the old line was opened again and it had to be closed just ten years later, for exactly the same reasons as it had been 120 years previously. However the old 19th Lock has been re-opened once more and the Old Barrow Line is now fully navigable again.

Ballyteague Castle is a typical example of the Irish fortified house of the 14th to 16th Century. It is thought to have been a "Geraldine" Castle (i.e. of the Fitzgerald dynasty) and Thomas Fitzgerald 10th Earl of Kildare, known as Silken Thomas, is said to have taken refuge here after the battle of Allen in 1535.

To the east is the Hill of Allen (203m) where Finn MacCool (Fionn MacCumhaill) is reputed to have lived. The tower is a folly erected about 1860 by one of the Alymer family on the site of a pre-historic tumulus.

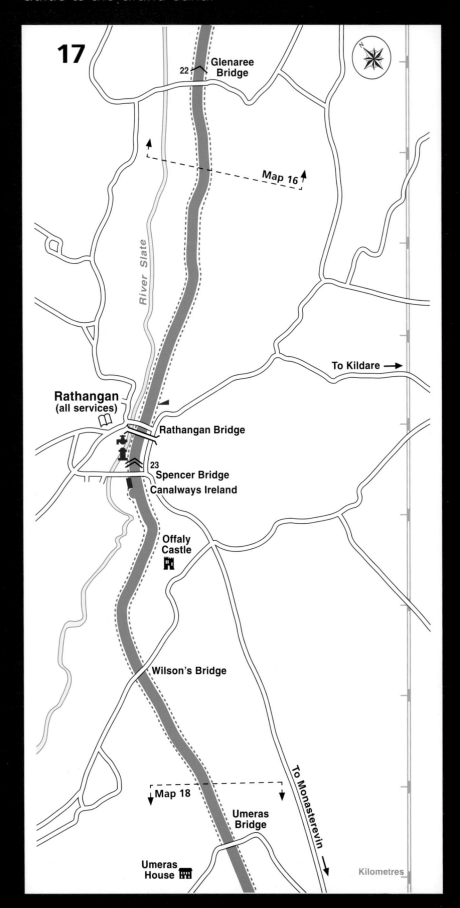

17

22 Glenaree Bridge

Map 16

River Slate

To Kildare →

Rathangan
(all services)

Rathangan Bridge

23 Spencer Bridge
Canalways Ireland

Offaly
Castle

Wilson's Bridge

Map 18

To Monasterevin

Umeras
Bridge

Umeras
House

Kilometres

SECTION 17 Glenaree Bridge to Umeras Bridge

Route Description

Once through Glenaree Bridge, the canal becomes more sheltered and some tree planting has been carried out. The spire of Rathangan church is clearly visible in the distance. The attractive old warehouse at the approach to Rathangan was destroyed by fire some years ago but the local people have made great efforts to improve the waterfront and there is convenient mooring between the bridges with good shopping facilities. The old harbour near the double lock is an indication that this was once a busy canal centre. There is a hire-boat base, Canalways Ireland, below 23rd Lock and Spencer Bridge. The Slate River, known as the little Barrow below Rathangan Bridge, closes with the canal here and the mounds raised when this river was dredged may be seen to the west.

Just north of Rathangan the canal is carried to an embankment above the level of the surrounding countryside. At the base of the embankment, on both sides of the canal, there are small areas of wetland. Many plant species grow here which are rarely found elsewhere along the canal system, including Grass-of-Parnassus and a number of different orchids.

Facilities

All Services: Rathangan
Water, Slip: Rathangan Bridge

History

The early engineers experienced difficulty with this stretch of canal as well as the bog section. Mistakes in the levels forced the company to turn Rathangan Lock into a double lock. Local contractors were employed under the supervision of the company engineer and there is a noticeable difference in the quality of the materials used in some of the bridges.

The ancient rath (fort), an imposing 54 metres in diameter, from which Rathangan takes its name, is still visible but Rathangan Castle was demolished in the 1760s. In the records of the company there is mention of the purchasing of land for the canal from James Spencer of Rathangan House in 1784. In 1798 the same Mr Spencer was piked to death in his house by insurgents but his name survives on the bridge. Two days later the insurgents under John Doorley were driven from the town and Doorley was killed. His death is recorded on the family tombstone in the local churchyard.

South of Spencer Bridge on the east bank there is a good example of a canal milestone. In 1783 the board ordered milestones in English miles (1609 metres) from James's Street Harbour to be placed on the north (or west) bank and in Irish miles (2048 metres) from Dublin Castle on the south (or east) bank.

A peat litter factory was set up at Umeras in 1885 attempting to utilise some of the turf in the area. Amongst other things experiments were tried in producing board from turf but without success. The factory continued under different owners until it was destroyed by fire in 1940 and today the remains of a quay and a few mooring posts are all that survive of this industrial activity.

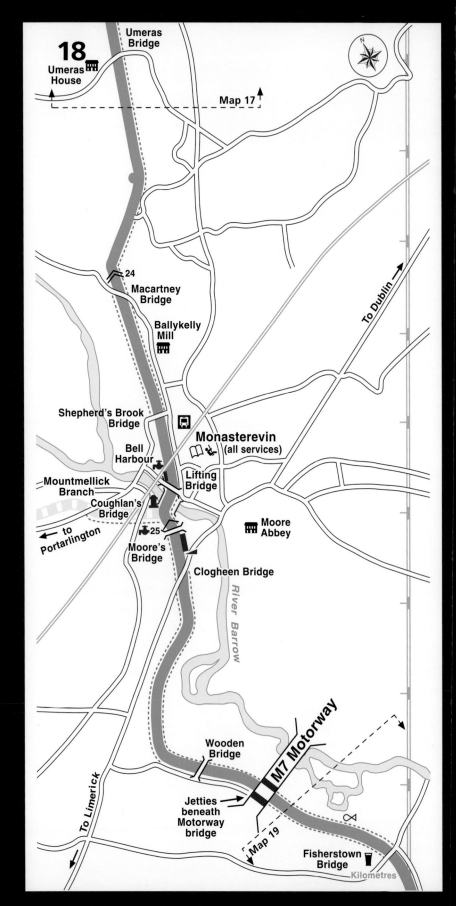

18

Umeras House

Umeras Bridge

24 Macartney Bridge

Ballykelly Mill

Shepherd's Brook Bridge

Bell Harbour

Mountmellick Branch

Coughlan's Bridge

← to Portarlington

Moore's Bridge

25

Monasterevin (all services)

Lifting Bridge

Moore Abbey

Clogheen Bridge

Map 17 ↑

To Dublin

River Barrow

Wooden Bridge

Jetties beneath Motorway bridge

M7 Motorway

Map 19

Fisherstown Bridge

To Limerick

Kilometres

SECTION 18   Umeras Bridge to Fisherstown Bridge

Route Description

Macartney Bridge and double lock form an attractive scene with whitewashed cottages. Passing Ballykelly Mill, founded in 1801, the canal approaches Monasterevin with its maze of waterways, roads and railways and its multiplicity of bridges, ancient and modern. One of these, a lifting bridge over the canal, must be opened before proceeding. In order to open the bridge the lockkeeper must be summoned from 24th or 25th Lock. Crossing the River Barrow by a fine aqueduct with three 12m spans, the canal turns to the south while the Mountmellick Branch, now derelict, veers off to the west. It is possible to walk to the first bridge over the branch, known locally as Coughlan's Bridge, after a family who lived nearby. Emerging from the 25th Lock and Moore's Bridge, the canal turns sharply and this bend can present problems when travelling towards Dublin with the bridge and lock appearing unexpectedly. The canal now approaches Clogheen Bridge which carries the old N7 road. This is a low flat span bridge. Some 3km further along is the M7 motorway bridge, where moorings are located on the north bank, beneath the bridge.

The canal now follows the line of the Barrow valley and there is a long level of 21km ahead.

Facilities

All Services: Monasterevin
Slip: Clogheen Bridge
Water: Moore's Bridge, Bell Harbour

History

Attention often focuses on the various ways of spelling Monasterevin, even among the local people. Some say the town derives its name from a monastery founded here by St Evin. The site of the ancient monastery is now occupied by Moore Abbey, built in 1607 and enlarged in 1846. For many years it was the seat of the Moores, Earls of Drogheda, and was subsequently the home of John Count McCormack before being purchased by the Sisters of Charity.

There is a wealth of local history connected with this town which was once the centre of several thriving industries, including Cassidy's distillery (1784-1934). A short branch canal formerly ran into the centre of the town and the old harbour area may still be traced. Bell Harbour, on the west side of the canal, was refurbished a number of years ago. Water is available here and the train station is only a short distance away.

It was originally intended that the navigation should enter the River Barrow here but it was subsequently decided to continue the still-water canal to Athy. In the early years the boats used to lock down into the river and up on the far side. The sites of these early locks are still visible. However, when the Mountmellick Branch was constructed in the 1820s, it was decided to do away with this unsatisfactory arrangement and the aqueduct and lifting bridge were erected. The Mountmellick Branch had originally been envisaged as a canal to the Castlecomer coal fields but all that was accomplished was the 18km to Mountmellick. By the 1950s it had almost ceased to be used and it was officially closed to navigation in 1960. The land was sold off, and many stretches, including the section through Portarlington, have now been filled in, so there is little hope of restoring this branch.

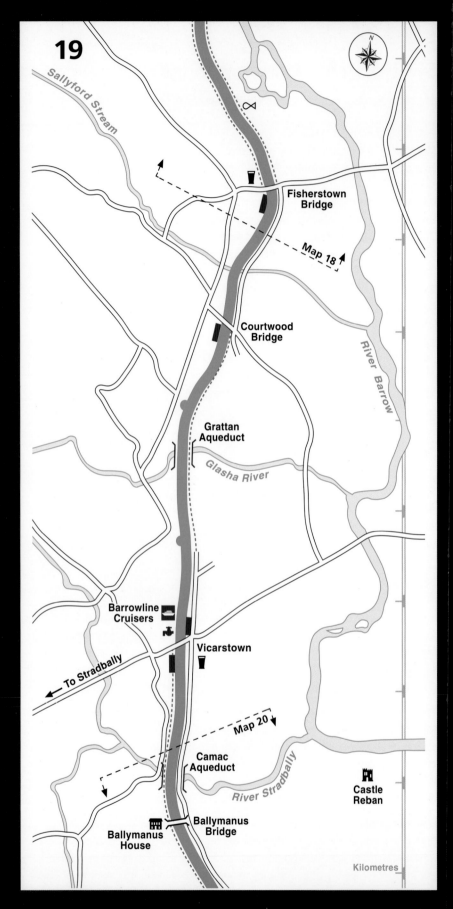

19

Sallyford Stream

Fisherstown Bridge

Map 18

River Barrow

Courtwood Bridge

Grattan Aqueduct

Glasha River

Barrowline Cruisers

Vicarstown

To Stradbally

Map 20

Camac Aqueduct

River Stradbally

Castle Reban

Ballymanus House

Ballymanus Bridge

Kilometres

SECTION 19   Fisherstown Bridge to Ballymanus Bridge

Route Description

In order to achieve the long level without a lock, the canal is now carried on an embankment to Fisherstown Bridge and then through a cutting to Courtwood Bridge. Vicarstown is an attractive village with friendly pubs on both sides of the canal. From here it is possible to walk about 1.5km to the east to Dunrally Castle and Bridge. The more energetic travellers might like to go to Stradbally 5km to the west where there is an interesting steam museum. There is a road along the canal all the way from Vicarstown to Athy.

Facilities

Pubs: Vicarstown and Fisherstown Bridge
(about 200m to the west of the bridge)
Water: Vicarstown

History

The canal from Monasterevin to Athy was constructed in the same way as the Main Line, with the work divided up into lots to be undertaken by local contractors. It was not until some time later that the larger canal contractors emerged, but it is interesting that one of the local

contractors on this stretch was John McMahon, co-founder of the first large civil engineering firm in the country. Both his partners, Bernard Mullins and David Henry, also started as small contractors working on the Grand Canal. Together as Henry, Mullins and McMahon, they were responsible for the construction of the Naas Branch of the Grand Canal from Naas to Corbally Harbour, the Ballinasloe and Mountmellick Branches, also part of the Grand Canal network, and for the Royal Canal from Coolnahay, west of Mullingar, to Richmond Harbour and the Shannon. At one time there were over 4,000 men at work on the Barrow Line. Again there were troubles with inaccurate surveys which caused errors in the levels. Omer's original estimate for the canal from Dublin to Athy had been £98,000 - the final cost was just under £500,000.

Ballymanus Bridge is heavily scored with rope marks made by the horsedrawn boats of the past as they turned the corner into the bridge.

Where the canal bends towards the River Barrow, Castle Reban is visible with Bert House on the nearby hill. Castle Reban was a 13th Century castle built on the site of an ancient town according to Ptolemy's map of the 2nd Century. Fynes Moryson, the famous traveller, passing through here in 1617 remarked, "I pass over...the ancient city of Reban, now a poor village with a castle". Today there is not even a village remaining and there is a private house beside the ruined castle.

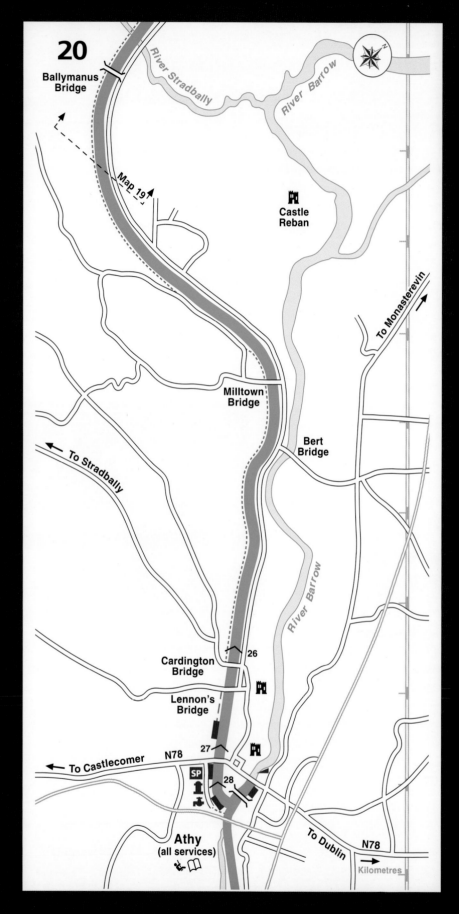

20

Ballymanus
Bridge

River Stradbally

River Barrow

N

Map 19

Castle
Reban

To Monasterevin

Milltown
Bridge

Bert
Bridge

To Stradbally

River Barrow

26

Cardington
Bridge

Lennon's
Bridge

27

To Castlecomer   N78

SP

28

Athy
(all services)

To Dublin   N78

Kilometres

SECTION 20 Ballymanus Bridge to Athy

Route Description

Glimpses of the Barrow increase as the canal and river near their junction at Athy. Care is required at Milltown Bridge by high air draft vessels owing to the design of the bridge.

In places the accompanying road swings slightly away from the canal creating an impression of isolation. There is a good view of the town as the canal drops down to the river level.

Before locking out through 28th Lock into the river, it is well worth looking at the attractive Horse Bridge spanning the river here. From it, looking upstream, there is a good view of the town with the interesting Dominican church with a paraboloid roof, erected in 1965. The River Barrow is navigable for a short distance upstream through Horse Bridge and there is a floating jetty just before the Town Bridge (Cromaboo Bridge). There is access to a slip on the east bank through the Town Bridge and there are mooring posts above the slip. Looking downstream the first of the river navigation's unguarded weirs may be seen beneath the railway bridge and on the east bank the entrance to the first of the navigation cuts. On emerging from the lock it is necessary to cross the river to enter this cut.

Facilities

All Services: Athy
Slip: Athy, in river, upstream of Dublin Road Bridge
Water, Pump-Out Station: Lock 28

History

From early times small boats have used the Barrow above Athy and even after the canal was completed they continued to do so to avoid the payment of tolls. There is evidence that at one time there was a lock just above Athy.

Athy (the ford of Ae) has been an important river crossing from early times and is full of historical interest. It has been the site of many battles from the time in the 11th Century when Ae, King of Leinster, fell here. In 1308 the

town was burned by the native Irish and seven years later it was again plundered, this time by the Scots under Robert Bruce. The Town Bridge was built in 1796 but the first recorded bridge on this site dates back to 1413. Beside the bridge is White's Castle, which was built in 1506 by the eighth Earl of Kildare. Seventy years later, it was enlarged by William White, hence its name. A short distance upstream is Woodstock Castle, built in the 13th Century and later taken over by the Fitzgeralds. According to tradition Thomas, the infant son of Maurice Fitzjohn Fitzgerald was rescued by a monkey when there was a fire in this castle and thereafter there has always been a monkey in the Kildare coat-of-arms.

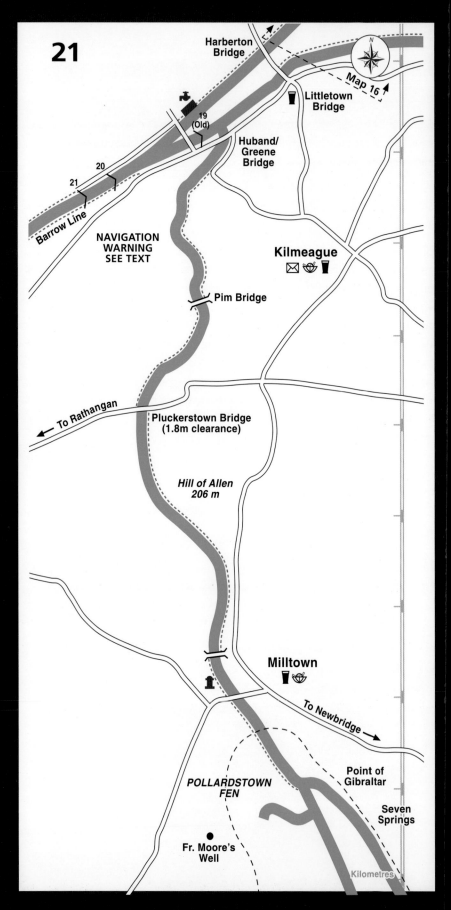

21

Harberton Bridge

Littletown Bridge

19 (Old)

Huband/ Greene Bridge

20

21

Barrow Line

NAVIGATION WARNING SEE TEXT

Kilmeague

Pim Bridge

To Rathangan

Pluckerstown Bridge (1.8m clearance)

Hill of Allen 206 m

Milltown

To Newbridge

Point of Gibraltar

POLLARDSTOWN FEN

Seven Springs

Fr. Moore's Well

Kilometres

Map 16

MAP & GUIDE 21 THE MILLTOWN FEEDER AND POLLARDSTOWN FEN

Route Description

The maximum size of craft that can navigate the Milltown Feeder is limited to 0.75m draft and 1.8m height over water line owing to restricted clearance at Pluckerstown Bridge. It is not possible to turn a craft of more than 7.5m at Pluckerstown. The limit of navigation is the Point of Gibraltar where there is ample room to turn.

Facilities

Shop, Pub, Post Office: Kilmeague
Shop, Pub: Milltown
Pub: Littletown Bridge
Water: 19th Lock (Old Barrow Line)

The Milltown Feeder

The Milltown Feeder, or as it is sometimes called, The Grand Supply, is the main source of water for the Grand Canal and the Barrow Line of the Grand Canal. It enters the summit level above the old 19th Lock near Lowtown. Passing close to the village of Kilmeague, it follows the natural contour around the Hill of Allen to Milltown Bridge, a total distance of about 10km from Lowtown. It continues into Pollardstown Fen, a further 3km to the Seven Springs, narrowing as it approaches the small pool with its bubbling springs of crystal clear water, also known as James's Well. In the late 18th Century further supplies were added to the main supply, drawing from the western side of the fen, an area around Father Moore's Well. There are 36 known springs in the whole area. There were originally three mills, at Pollardstown, Milltown and Pluckerstown, also drawing on this excellent supply and so the whole area is most confusing with old millraces, streams and drains, some natural and some artificial.

Pollardstown Fen

Pollardstown Fen is the largest remaining spring-fed fen in Ireland (over 235 ha) and is of international importance. Accordingly it is designated as a Special Area of Conservation (SAC) under the EU Habitats directive. It contains a number of rare vegetation types and invertebrates, along with an uninterrupted pollen record of the changes in the composition of its vegetation going back to the last ice age. Fens gradually evolved from shallow lakes but most of them subsequently became covered by raised bogland. Pollardstown survived because the great quantities of lime-rich alkaline waters from the springs preserved the water table and retained the right conditions for it to remain as a fen.

Pollardstown Fen contains many different plants and vegetation types, some rare and others less so, including Saw-Sedge, Black Bog-Rush, Purple Moorgrass, Common Reed, Fen Rush, Fen Bog-Cotton, Fen Sedge, Hemp Agrimony, Angelica and Fen Thistle. Of particular interest are the insectivorous plants (Butterwort and Bladderwort) and the orchids (Fragrant Orchid, Fly Orchid and the Marsh Orchids). The Fen provides a habitat for many wildfowl and insects and is home of a small rare snail (Vertigo geyeri). Mammals that live on the fen include Otters, Hares and Pygmy Shrews.

Visitors should not wander outside the fenced areas of the Fen – it can be very dangerous because of the wet ground and many deep drains.

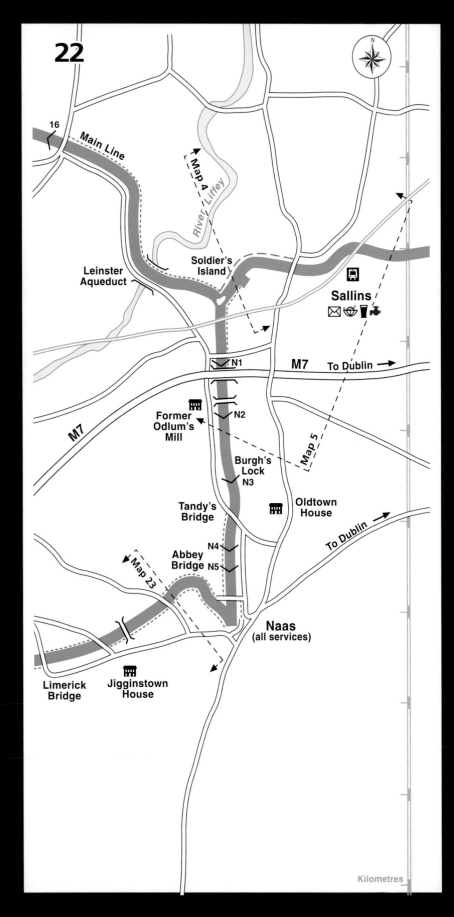

22

16

Main Line

River Liffey

Map 4

Leinster
Aqueduct

Soldier's
Island

Sallins

N1

M7   To Dublin →

M7

Former
Odlum's
Mill

N2

Map 5

Burgh's
Lock
N3

Tandy's
Bridge

Oldtown
House

N4
To Dublin →

Abbey
Bridge   N5

Map 23

Naas
(all services)

Limerick
Bridge

Jigginstown
House

Kilometres

MAPS & GUIDES 22 & 23
THE NAAS AND CORBALLY BRANCH

SECTION 22   Soldier's Island
to Naas Harbour

Route Description

The Naas Branch enters the Main Line of the canal at Soldier's Island, between Sallins and Leinster Aqueduct (Section 5). It extends southwards for about 4km to Naas Harbour and is a most attractive stretch of waterway surrounded by woodland and lined by fine beech trees. It is possible to drive along the canal for almost its entire length. Between 1st Lock, Osbertstown Bridge, and 2nd Lock at Odlum's Mills the canal is crossed by the N7 & Naas Ring Road. It continues on through Burgh Lock and Tandy's Bridge at Oldtown, past the old Naas gasworks between 4th and 5th Locks, before passing under Abbey (or Finlay) Bridge to enter the harbour at Naas.

Facilities

All Services: Naas
Post Office, Shop, Pub, Water: Sallins

History

The County of Kildare Canal Company was set up in 1786 by local landowners to construct a canal to Naas. The canal was completed in 1789 and work was commenced on an extension to Kilcullen and Co Wicklow, but the company was heavily in debt and entered into negotiations with the Grand Canal Company to sell out. No agreement was reached and eventually, in 1807, the Grand Canal Company bought the concern from the Court of Chancery for a mere £2,250. The three Naas Canal bridges were rebuilt with increased headroom. This was unfortunate because the original bridges built by the engineer, William Chapman, were skew bridges crossing the canal at an angle. The techniques for building humpbacked skew bridges, which involved complicated lines in the courses of the stonework, had been worked out by the Romans, but Chapman's Naas Canal bridges were the first examples of this type of bridge in these islands. Some traces of the old abutments can still be seen. A feature of Chapman's lock design was the introduction of land racks with the water discharging into the lock from beneath the upper cill.

The old canal store at Naas Harbour (now used by a local youth group) and the Earl of Mayo's fine Market House nearby, built in 1813, are an indication of the thriving trade which existed in the past. A passenger boat also operated on this line for a period. Traffic declined from the turn of the century. Reeve's Mill and Maltings at Athgarvan ceased to use the Corbally Extension but Odlum's Mills, which date back to 1790, continued to operate its own fleet of boats on the canal until the 1940s and accepted CIE's decision to withdraw the commercial boats with reluctance. The canal was officially closed to navigation in 1961 but pressure to have it restored began in the 1970s.

The re-opening of the branch from Soldier's Island to Naas in 1987 was the first major restoration project undertaken by The Office of Public Works following the transfer of the canals from CIE. The five locks are now in full working order and the line to Naas Harbour is navigable again.

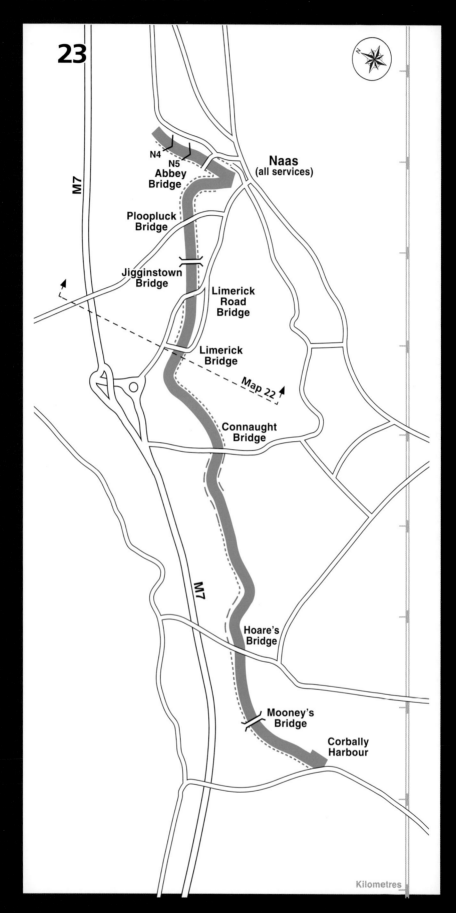

23

N4
N5
Abbey
Bridge

Naas
(all services)

Ploopluck
Bridge

Jigginstown
Bridge

Limerick
Road
Bridge

Limerick
Bridge

Map 22

Connaught
Bridge

M7

M7

Hoare's
Bridge

Mooney's
Bridge

Corbally
Harbour

Kilometres

SECTION 23   Naas Harbour to Corbally Harbour

Route Description

The Corbally Extension of the Naas Branch is 8km long, without any locks. A low level bridge just outside Naas, built in the early 1950s, prevents boats from travelling west to Corbally Harbour. It is hoped that the future may see this navigation obstruction resolved and

Photo courtesy: Giles Byford

the branch restored to navigation. The banks do, however, offer an interesting walk from Naas Harbour to Corbally for the hardy walker, although they can become very wet in winter and overgrown in summer. Walkers must come prepared to negotiate fences across the path, and should be aware of the proximity of cattle in open fields adjoining the canal banks.

The channel, unlike many of the disused branches, has not been allowed to dry out, and it supports a wide variety of aquatic plants. The reason the channel remains in water is because the water supply for the entire Naas and Corbally Branch enters the canal at Corbally Harbour, and flows from there to Naas and then down through the five falling locks to the Main Line at Soldier's Island.

Facilities

All Services: Naas

History

When the Grand Canal Company bought the canal after the Kildare Canal Company went bankrupt, extensive repairs had to be carried out to make the structures conform with those on the Grand Canal itself. Between 1808 and 1810 the branch line was extended to Corbally where the ruins of old canal buildings can still be seen. However, plans to extend it into Co Wicklow were abandoned, even though the engineer John Killaly did survey a route through Kilcullen and Baltinglas.

The Corbally Extension was built not by an individual contractor, or even by a number of contractors working simultaneously, which had been the way canals were built up until then. It was the first contract undertaken by the civil engineering firm of Henry, Mullins & McMahon (see Section 19).

The ruins of Jigginstown House and 16th Century Castle Rag near the low level bridge on the Corbally Extension are well worth a visit. Jigginstown was a grand mansion built for the Lord Deputy, Thomas Wentworth, Earl of Strafford, in about 1637 to entertain his monarch, Charles I, and for use as a country residence for the Lord Deputy. It was never completed but it remains a fine example of early architecture and brick work.

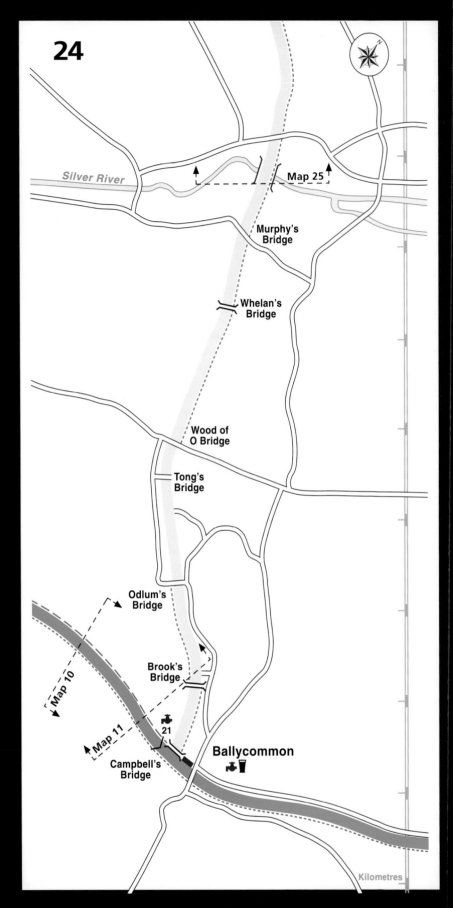

24

Silver River

Map 25

Murphy's
Bridge

Whelan's
Bridge

Wood of
O Bridge

Tong's
Bridge

Odlum's
Bridge

Map 10

Brook's
Bridge

21

Map 11

Ballycommon

Campbell's
Bridge

Kilometres

MAPS & GUIDES 24 & 25
THE KILBEGGAN BRANCH

SECTION 24   Campbell's Bridge
to Murphy's Bridge

Route Description

The Kilbeggan Branch enters the Main Line of the canal at Ballycommon, between Daingean and Tullamore (Section 10). There are no locks on the Kilbeggan Branch. A dam was built across the mouth of the branch when it was closed to navigation in 1961 and the branch line was drained into the Silver River by manually cutting a small drainage channel from the canal.

Significant work has been done by the Kilbeggan Harbour Amenity Group to restore the canal branch walks. It is possible to walk from Ballycommon to Kilbeggan along the banks of the disused canal - a distance of 13km through scrub and grassland, across a raised bog and past esker ridges (mounds of sand and gravel left by the retreating glaciers after the last Ice Age). The paths can be overgrown in summer and very wet in winter, but for the hardy walker they offer an interesting walk with a wide range of scenery. All walkers should come prepared for the following:

*   Be aware of the proximity of cattle in the open fields adjoining the canal banks.

*   Come prepared to negotiate any fences you may find across the towpath.

*   Remember that conditions are likely to be muddy and wet, and that the route is not sign-posted.

The campaign to restore the Kilbeggan Branch to full navigation continues. The Ballycommon Canal Renewal Group was formed in 2009 to promote and restore the Ballycommon end of the line. Their work continues with numerous work parties. Offaly IWAI supports both these community groups and the campaign they lead.

Facilities

Pub, Water: Ballycommon Bridge
Water: Lock 21

History

The idea of building a canal to Kilbeggan was put forward in 1796. In spite of being invited to do so by a group of local landowners, the Grand Canal Company did not feel that building this branch was a sound business proposition. In 1806 it was suggested that a narrow canal should be built instead. The Grand Canal Company offered to pay the difference in cost if the new canal were built to conform with the existing line, but nothing was done this time either. In 1827, encouraged by its success in getting loans to finance other branches, the Grand Canal Company applied for a loan to build a canal to Kilbeggan. The loan was approved, but the Royal Canal Company lodged a complaint that the new canal would interfere with its trade. The loan approval was withdrawn, but authorised again in 1828, after extensive negotiations. Work on the canal began in 1830.

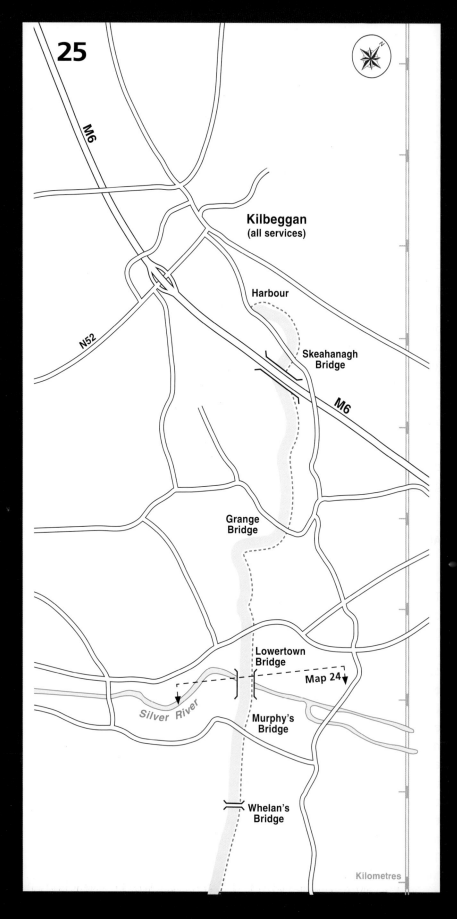

25

Kilbeggan
(all services)

Harbour

Skeahanagh
Bridge

M6

N52

Grange
Bridge

Lowertown
Bridge

Map 24

Silver River

Murphy's
Bridge

Whelan's
Bridge

Kilometres

SECTION 25   Murphy's Bridge
to Kilbeggan Harbour

Route Description

The Kilbeggan Harbour Amenity Group has done a marvellous job in restoring the old harbour building. This was completed with the assistance of a FAS scheme in the early 1990s. This was an enormous undertaking as the buildings were in a very derelict condition at that time. The buildings are now used as office premises. The harbour was dredged by the Office of Public Works at the same time. However no feeder streams enter the Kilbeggan Branch, which has to be fed from the Main Line, and so the harbour is still dry.

The wildlife of the Kilbeggan Branch is very diverse. The channel was cut through a number of eskers and also crosses a raised bog. Plants growing on eskers have to be tolerant of very calcareous or lime-rich conditions. On raised bogs the soil is very acidic and a different range of plants can be found. When the canal was being built across the bog, lime-rich soil was brought in to build up the towpath. As a result lime-loving plants such as Quaking Grass and Canine Thistle can now be found growing beside acid-loving species such as Purple Moor-grass and Bog Asphodel.

Because of the work done by the Kilbeggan Harbour Amenity Group to restore the canal branch walks, the harbour end of the canal bank now features a golden mile walk.

Facilities
All Services: Kilbeggan

History

The contractor who built the Kilbeggan Branch of the Grand Canal was William Dargan, who had just taken over the contract for the construction of the Ulster Canal which was being built at the same time. Dargan, a native of Carlow, had trained as an engineer and surveyor under Thomas Telford on the Holyhead Road. He went on to become one of Ireland's foremost railway engineers, involved in almost every railway built in the country, including the first, the Dublin and Kingstown Railway which opened in December 1834. There is a statue of Dargan in front of the National Gallery of Ireland on Merrion Square in Dublin.

William Dargan was, according to his contract, supposed to complete the canal in one year. In fact it was not opened to traffic until January 1835, four and a half years after work began. Even then the depth of water was still not satisfactory, and Dargan had to continue to maintain and improve the canal until February 1836. The delays were caused largely by problems in staunching the embankments on either side of the Silver River Aqueduct, on the Offaly and Westmeath county boundary.

DISTANCE TABLE km

GRAND CANAL MAIN LINE
Distance from Sea Lock at Ringsend to:-

	km
Westmoreland Sea Lock, Ringsend	0.0
McMahon Bridge, Ringsend	0.6
Maquay Bridge & Lock C1, Grand Canal St.	1.2
McKenny Bridge & Lock C2, Lower Mount St.	1.4
Huband Bridge & Lock C3, Upper Mount St.	1.6
Macartney Bridge & Lock C4, Baggot St.	2.0
Eustace Bridge & Lock C5, Leeson St.	2.6
Charlemont Bridge & Lock C6	3.2
La Touche Bridge & Lock C7, Portobello	3.6
Emmet Bridge, Harold's Cross	4.2
Parnell Bridge	4.6
Camac Bridge, Dolphin's Barn	5.0
Harberton Bridge	5.4
Griffith Bridge, junction with Main Line, 1st Lock, Suir Road Bridge	6.0
2nd Lock, Goldenbridge Footbridge	6.6
3rd Lock, Blackhorse Bridge, Inchicore	7.6
4th Lock	8.0
5th Lock	8.4
Kylemore Road Bridge	8.6
6th Lock	8.8
7th Lock, Ballyfermot Bridge	9.6
8th Lock	10.4
M50 Bridge	11.2
9th Lock, Clondalkin Bridge	12.2
10th Lock	12.6
11th Lock	13.0
12th Lock, Lucan Road Bridge	16.0
Gollierstown Bridge	17.4
Hazelhatch Bridge	20.6
Aylmer's Bridge	22.4
13th Lock	23.4
Henry Bridge	24.6
Ponsonby Bridge	27.0
14th Lock, Devonshire Bridge	29.4
15th Lock	30.0
Railway Bridge	32.0
Sallins Bridge	33.2
Junction with Naas Line	34.0
Leinster Aqueduct	35.0

DISTANCE TABLE

	km
16th Lock, Digby Bridge	37.2
17th Lock, Landenstown Bridge	38.2
18th Lock	39.6
Burgh or Cock Bridge	40.8
Bonynge or Healy's Bridge	42.6
Binn's Bridge, Robertstown	44.8
19th Lock, Lowtown & Lowtown Marina	46.2
Junction with new Barrow Line	46.4
Bond Bridge, Allenwood	48.0
Shee or Scow Bridge	49.4
Light Railway Bridge (lifting)	51.0
Hamilton Bridge	53.2
Bord na Móna Bridge, Kilpatrick	54.4
Hartley Bridge, Ticknevin	56.6
20th Lock, Ticknevin	57.4
Blundell Aqueduct. The Tunnel	62.0
Downshire Bridge, Edenderry Line	63.8
Colgan's Bridge	64.2
George's Bridge	64.4
Rathmore Bridge	65.2
Cartland Bridge	66.8
Trimblestown Bridge	68.8
Rhode Bridge	73.2
Toberdaly Bridge	74.2
Light Railway Bridge (lifting)	75.8
Killeen Bridge	78.8
Molesworth Bridge, Daingean	81.4
Bord na Móna Bridge (fixed span)	84.4
Chenevix Bridge, Ballycommon	86.8
Campbell's Bridge, over Kilbeggan Line	87.0
21st Lock, Ballycommon	87.2
22nd Lock, Cappyroe Bridge	88.6
23rd Lock	89.2
24th Lock	92.2
25th Lock, Cappincur Bridge	92.8
26th Lock	93.6
Bury Bridge, over Tullamore Harbour junction	95.0
Kilbeggan Road Bridge, Tullamore	95.4
27th Lock, Cox's Bridge	95.8
28th Lock	96.2
New Bridge	96.4

DISTANCE TABLE	km
Railway Bridge	96.6
Shra Bridge	97.8
29th Lock, Ballycowan Bridge	99.6
Huband Aqueduct	100.0
Charleville Aqueduct	101.0
Corcoran's Bridge, Rahan	103.6
Becan's Bridge, Rahan	104.8
Henesy's Bridge	105.8
30th Lock, Ballincloughin Bridge	106.6
31st Lock, Cornalour Bridge	107.4
Plunkett Bridge, Pollagh	111.0
Light Railway Bridge (swivel)	115.4
Derry Bridge	116.4
Macartney Aqueduct, Silver River	118.6
Armstrong Bridge, Gallen	121.6
Noggus Bridge	122.2
32nd Lock, Glyn Bridge	123.0
Judge's Bridge	124.2
33rd Lock, Belmont Bridge	125.0
L'Estrange Bridge	127.6
34th Lock, Clononey Bridge	128.6
Griffith Bridge, Shannon Harbour	130.0
35th Lock	130.6
36th Lock, junction with Shannon	131.0

DISTANCE TABLE	km
BARROW LINE OF GRAND CANAL	
Distance from junction with Main Line at Lowtown to:-	
Littletown Bridge	1.4
Ballyteague Bridge	2.8
20th Lock, Ballyteague	3.4
21st Lock, Ballyteague	3.6
22nd Lock, Glenaree Bridge	8.4
Rathangan Bridge	12.4
23rd Lock, Spencer Bridge and Canalways Ireland	13.2
Wilson's Bridge	15.4
Umeras Bridge	17.8
24th Lock, Macartney's Bridge	20.8
Shepherd's Brook or High Bridge	22.2
Monasterevin lifting bridge and Barrow Aqueduct	23.0
Junction with Mountmellick Branch	23.2

DISTANCE TABLE

	km
25th Lock, Moore's Bridge	23.4
Clogheen Bridge, Dublin Road	24.0
Old Bridge	26.4
Fisherstown Bridge	29.2
Courtwood Bridge	31.0
Grattan Aqueduct	32.6
Vicarstown Bridge	34.8
Camac Aqueduct	36.2
Ballymanus Bridge	36.8
Milltown Bridge	41.0
26th Lock, Cardington Bridge	44.4
Lennon's Bridge	44.6
27th Lock, Athy and Augustus Bridge	45.2
28th Lock, junction with River Barrow	45.6

DISTANCE TABLE

KILBEGGAN BRANCH

Distance from junction with Main Line at Ballycommon to:-

	km
Campbell's Bridge	0.0
Brook's Bridge	1.0
Odlum's Bridge	2.2
Tong's Bridge	3.5
Wood of O Bridge	4.0
Whelan's Bridge	6.1
Murphy's Bridge	6.9
Lowertown Bridge	8.2
Grange Bridge	10.1
Skeahanagh Bridge	12.5
Kilbeggan Harbour	13.1

THE INLAND WATERWAYS ASSOCIATION OF IRELAND

The Inland Waterways Association of Ireland is a voluntary body of inland waterways enthusiasts. We advocate the use, maintenance, protection, restoration and improvement of the inland waterways of Ireland. The association was founded in 1954 to campaign for the conservation and development of the waterways and in particular their preservation as working navigations. When the Shannon was almost totally undeveloped for pleasure boating, IWAI fought the building of low bridges, thus ensuring the development of the river as an asset for all to use and enjoy. In the 1960s IWAI successfully fought plans to close the Circular line of the Grand Canal in Dublin. Later the association campaigned for the re-opening of the Ballinamore & Ballyconnell Canal (now the Shannon-Erne Waterway) and the Naas line of the Grand Canal.

IWAI is the voice of waterways users and enthusiasts. It represents the views of members to governments (Northern Ireland & Ireland), to Waterways Ireland and other navigation authorities, to local authorities and the range of statutory and state-sponsored bodies whose activities impinge on the waterways in one way or another.

Membership and Organisation

IWAI has over 4,500 members mainly organised in branches associated with the major navigations across the island.

Our membership is drawn from all walks of life and from people with a wide range of interests - boating, angling, walking, heritage and environment. Many of our members own and use boats on our rivers, lakes and canals ranging from motor cruisers to jet-skis, from barges to sailing dinghies and RIBs to rowing boats.

The association is a company limited by guarantee and a registered charity (CHY no 10915). It is governed by a council made up of representatives of each of the local branches and directly elected officers and members. Day to day affairs are managed by an executive committee.

IWAI is not responsible for the navigation, for registering boats, for harbours or similar facilities. The authority that is responsible for the Shannon, Suck, Erne, Barrow, Lower Bann, Grand Canal, Royal Canal and Shannon-Erne Waterway is Waterways Ireland.

Publications: The IWAI publishes "Inland Waterways news", a quarterly magazine, sent out free to all members. The magazine covers a wide range of topics of interest to waterways enthusiasts at local, national and international level. IWAI also publishes a number of waterways related books and guides. Our website is one of the largest single reference sources for waterways related material in Ireland and a major source of referrals for waterways related businesses, which brings local events, activities and developments into national perspective. Some of the branches bring out local newsletters. Our website at **www.iwai.ie** is packed with waterways-related information. Whether a boat enthusiast, historian, archaeologist, or fisherman, you will find something here of interest.

Branches: IWAI has 21 branches: five in Northern Ireland, 14 in the Republic and two activity-based branches. Every member is affiliated to a local branch and each branch is represented on a national Council. The branches are:

Northern Ireland: Lough Erne, River Bann and Lough Neagh, Coalisland, Lagan and Newry

Ireland: Athlone, Barrow, Belturbet, Boyle River, Boyne Navigation, Carrick-on-Shannon, Corrib, Dublin, Kildare, Lough Derg, North Barrow, Offaly, Shannon Harbour, and Slaney

Activity-based: Cruising Club and Powerboat

There are four branches of IWAI active on the Grand Canal:

Dublin Branch	**www.dublin.iwai.ie**
Kildare Branch	**www.kildare.iwai.ie**
Offaly	**www.offaly.iwai.ie**
Shannon Harbour	**www.shr.iwai.ie**

You can join whichever branch you wish. You can join on line at **www.iwai.ie/join**

Improvements & Restoration: Work parties and funds are raised to improve navigations and to restore derelict ones. Current projects include the Ulster Canal, Lagan Navigation, Coalisland Canal, Boyne Navigation and the Kilbeggan and Corbally Lines of the Grand Canal.

Boat Rallies: IWAI organises rallies and other events including annual rallies on the Barrow (Easter), Dublin (May), the Erne (May), the Grand Canal (May & June), Shannon Harbour (June), the Corrib (July), the Shannon (July), Lough Derg (July). Competitions help to raise standards of boatmanship, seaworthiness and safety afloat.

Social Events: Land-based events such as film shows, discussions and lectures are organised on a range of waterways topics including, safety, vessel maintenance, navigation, first-aid and waterways heritage.

Member Services: IWAI provides a number of branded products and services for members. The association burgee and ensign are shown below. We also sell waterways-related books and navigation charts.

Email Discussion Forum: Why not sign up for our waterways mailing list discussion group at **www.iwai.ie/forum**. There you will meet folk who enjoy talking about life on our waterways. Generally, people are very free with advice on the list (whether wanted or not) and can point you in the right direction if you have problems finding a 3/4 inch flux capacitor for your 1904 vintage submarine!

Navigation and related announcements: If you would like to keep up to speed with announcements, news, and press releases from the IWAI, you can subscribe to the association's news updates list at **www.iwai.ie**

WATERWAYS IRELAND

Mission Statement

Waterways Ireland is the guardian of Ireland's inland navigations. Our mission is to provide a high quality recreational environment centred on the inland waterways of Ireland in our care, for the use and benefit of everyone.

Background

Waterways Ireland, the largest of the six north/south Implementation Bodies, is responsible for the management, maintenance, development and restoration of the specified inland navigable waterways, principally for recreational purposes. It is currently responsible for the following waterways:-

- Barrow Navigation
- Erne System
- Grand Canal
- Lower Bann Navigation
- Royal Canal
- Shannon-Erne Waterway
- Shannon Navigation

Waterways Ireland's remit was extended in 2007 by the North/South Ministerial Council, to include responsibility for the restoration of the section of the Ulster Canal between Clones and Upper Lough Erne, and, following restoration, for the management, maintenance, and development of this waterway principally for recreational purposes. Waterways Ireland was established under the British Irish Agreement in 1999.

Funding

Waterways Ireland is funded jointly by both jurisdictions, with 15% of current funding provided by the Northern Ireland Assembly and 85% by the Irish Government, reflecting the present distribution of the navigable waterways. Capital development programmes are funded separately in each jurisdiction. Waterways Ireland continues to progress works under Ireland's National Development Plan (NDP), as part of its waterways programme. It also carries out a separate capital development programme in Northern Ireland funded by the Department of Culture, Arts and Leisure (DCAL).

Organisation

Waterways Ireland Headquarters is based at 2 Sligo Road, Enniskillen, Co Fermanagh. The waterways are divided into three regions:-

Eastern - Royal and Grand Canals and Barrow Navigation;
Western - Shannon Navigation and
Northern - Shannon-Erne Waterway, Erne System and Lower Bann Navigation.

Regional Offices are located at Dublin, Scarriff and Carrick-on-Shannon respectively. There are also several depots and offices along the various navigations.